The War Diary of Asha-san

From Tokyo to Netaji's Indian National Army

Lt Bharati 'Asha' Sahay Choudhry

Translated by Tanvi Srivastava

HarperCollins *Publishers* India

First published in hardback in India in 2022
by HarperCollins *Publishers*
4th Floor, Tower A, Building No. 10, Phase II, DLF Cyber City,
Gurugram, Haryana – 122002
www.harpercollins.co.in

This edition published in India by HarperCollins Publishers 2023

2 4 6 8 10 9 7 5 3 1

P-ISBN: 978-93-5699-577-2
E-ISBN: 978-93-5629-146-1

Typeset in 11.5/15 Adobe Caslon Pro
Manipal Technologies Limited, Manipal

Printed and bound at
Thomson Press (India) Ltd

The War Diary of Asha-san

'Lt Bharati "Asha" Sahay Choudhry—Asha-san in her first home in Japan—tells the gripping story of her unusual life. As the eldest daughter of a couple of Indian expatriate freedom fighters, she had burned with the desire to fight for the independence of her faraway motherland, India. She was allowed to leave her war-torn first home, Japan, to join the Rani of Jhansi Regiment of the Indian National Army by her commander-in-chief Netaji Subhas Chandra Bose, at the age of only seventeen, in March 1945. After the defeat of the Indian National Army in August 1945, she came to India in 1946, where she made her new home in the country to which she had devoted her love and her wish to sacrifice everything. With her indomitable spirit she is a true Rani of Jhansi in her ripe age.'

— ANITA BOSE PFAFF, daughter of Netaji Subhas Chandra Bose

'Bharati "Asha" Sahay's war diary is a deeply moving first-hand account of the patriotic fervour of the Azad Hind movement led by Netaji Subhas Chandra Bose as seen through the eyes of an idealistic teenager as she travelled from Japan via Taiwan to Thailand to join the Rani of Jhansi Regiment. It documents the dramatic impact of the saga of Netaji and the INA on the Indian people in the aftermath of World War II, as she travels across India with her father Anand Mohan Sahay and is eventually reunited with her mother Sati Sen in 1947. This evocative translation of a diary originally written in Japanese will be an inspiration for the younger generation of Indians on the 75th anniversary of independence.'

— SUGATA BOSE, Gardiner Professor of Oceanic History and Affairs, Harvard University, and author of *His Majesty's Opponent: Subhas Chandra Bose and India's Struggle Against Empire*

'A valuable first-hand account of an important part of history, still relatively untold, when the struggle for Indian independence crossed paths with the war in the Far East. Asha-san's memoirs bring out her love for Japan, as well as her fierce love for India, and provide a cultural cross-reference that is not available in Allied accounts of the Second World War. Seen through the unfiltered lens of a seventeen-year-old who signs up for the Rani of Jhansi Regiment, it is a glimpse into the leadership of Subhas Chandra Bose in the Far East and the organization of the INA. This translation will bring a complicated story to a wider readership. It shows that the narrative of war and independence is never black-and-white, and not always the one told by the victors.'

— SHRABANI BASU, author of *Victoria & Abdul: The True Story of the Queen's Closest Confidant*

'This is a beautiful, engrossing book that I wholeheartedly recommend to every Indian. The role of militant women in national liberation struggles is forgotten all too soon, and they become mere footnotes in history. Lt Bharati "Asha" Sahay Choudhry, of the Rani of Jhansi Regiment of the Indian National Army, is a historical figure in our nation's freedom struggle, and this memoir, in her own words, makes for exhilarating reading. It is humorous (as when she learns Hindi) and exciting (as when she learns to fire a machine gun)—and I urge you to pick up this brilliant memoir.'

— MEENA KANDASAMY, author of *When I Hit You: Or, A Portrait of the Writer as a Young Wife*

Praveer,

This diary is for you. Didn't you say, 'Ma, I will serve the nation even more than you?'

So what if you couldn't fulfil your wish in this life? Life after life, you will be reborn as a patriot, the jewel of India.

Inspire those who follow you…

—Ma

CONTENTS

THE SETTING

Based on the memoirs of Anand Mohan Sahay[1]

Foremost, this is a love story.

It is December 1920. Anand Mohan Sahay, a second-year student at Patna's Temple Medical School, arrives at a large park with his classmates. Vast crowds huddle together as a wintery chill descends from the plains in the northwest. The students jostle past men and women to reach the dais. Standing before them is the renowned leader of the Indian National Congress, Mahatma Gandhi. Gandhi repositions a hand-spun woollen shawl over his shoulder and clears his throat. His speech, like his demeanour, is simple: he appeals to students to give up their studies and join the struggle for freedom. He asks government officers and lawyers to resign. If the people of India respond to his call of non-violent non-cooperation, India will be free within a year.

Anand returns to his narrow hostel room and lies awake in bed. Gandhi's words have stirred his imagination. Agitated, he turns to his roommate but finds him sound asleep. The next morning, he organizes a student meeting on campus. Anand is a striking man, with a firm mouth, determined eyes and prominent ears. As he runs a hand through his thick hair, all eyes turn to him. He is motivated to join Gandhi's movement, he says, but cannot accept the time frame. How can India be free within a year? The others concur. They ask him to approach Dr Rajendra Prasad, the well-known Congress leader from Bihar. Rajendra Babu promptly introduces Anand to Gandhi.

Gandhi reiterates his message—the British government will be paralysed if the people of India stop cooperating. Self-rule, or swaraj, can be attained non-violently. Anand is still in disbelief. He asks: Can a doctor stop treating his patient? Can he allow his patient to die? What change can happen in a year? Gandhi initially answers the questions patiently, but gradually grows blunt: 'Don't you realize that humanity is starving and slowly dying in India? Are you prepared to lay down your life for your country? If you are prepared, then where does the question of time arise?'

The next morning, Anand drops out of medical school. He joins Dr Rajendra Prasad as his private secretary and dedicates his life to India's freedom.

***

A year later, Edward VIII, the Prince of Wales, arrives in Calcutta for Christmas. He is on a reluctant four-month tour of India. His job—to save the Empire. Edward is a slight man with light blond hair and a seemingly shy demeanour. Over the last month, he's been travelling across India to thank the rulers of princely states for their support during the Great War. But while the prince attends lavish dinner parties and polo matches, rioters and protestors march through the streets. Calcutta is no different. As his carriage turns towards the striking Government House at the corner of Old Court Street, he sees a protest in the distance: thousands of women dressed in hand-spun cotton sarees marching with the Indian National Congress flag in their hands. He learns they are singing songs of freedom, exhorting the people of India to boycott foreign goods and textiles. The British government had promised India progressive self-rule for its support during the war. Not only did this promise remain unfulfilled, but the horrific massacre at Jallianwala Bagh in 1919 highlighted the callousness of the administration. By 1921, Indian nationalism had risen to a fever pitch with millions heeding Gandhi's call for non-cooperation.

Sati Sen, a slender figure with a long petulant face and blazing eyes, is one of these young women rallying on the streets of Calcutta. She marches barefoot to Presidency Jail, chanting a cry for her motherland—'Bande Mataram'. The British have arrested her mother, Urmila Devi, sister of Chittaranjan Das, the reputed Congress leader, as well as her aunt, Basanti Devi, the wife of Chittaranjan Das. They have charged the women with selling banned khadi—hand-spun natural fibre cloth—and organizing a strike to protest the arrival of the prince. Sati Sen and hundreds of others offer themselves up for arrest in protest.

***

Less than two months later, everything changes. On 4 February 1922, protestors gather at a market in Chauri Chaura, a small town two hundred and fifty kilometres northwest of Patna. They are volunteers of Gandhi's non-cooperation movement, picketing a liquor shop and shouting anti-British slogans. Armed local police grow nervous and fire shots in the air. The protest soon turns violent. There is escalation on both sides and the ensuing violence kills three civilians and over twenty policemen. One week later, a stricken Mahatma Gandhi calls off the non-cooperation movement at the national level. He cannot tolerate such violence. Millions of Indians, including young men like Anand, reel in shock. Freedom—almost within their grasp—is once again a distant dream.

***

Another year passes. It is December 1922. An extensive field is being cleared beside a mango orchard near Gaya, a hundred kilometres south of Patna. Not too far from the meandering Phalgu river, a large bamboo structure is being erected. It will soon be draped with white, green and saffron strips of hand-spun khadi. Anand pushes back his windswept hair and frowns as he observes the preparations; they are far behind schedule. Delegates will arrive for the 37th Annual Session of the Indian National Congress in two days. The grounds have still not been levelled. Unlike the previous session in Ahmedabad, preparations this time have been chaotic: Bihar is a poor province and funds are difficult to raise, especially with the threat of widespread arrests. Prominent leaders, such as Mahatma Gandhi, are in prison and communal riots have broken out in Punjab. Dr Rajendra Prasad, one of the few leaders who remains free, has had to rush to Multan to restore peace. Upon his return to Bihar, work for the annual Congress session proceeds at a manic pace.

At the opening session, Anand encounters national leaders like Chittaranjan Das, better known as Deshbandhu or 'Friend of the Nation'. Das is the president-elect of the Indian National Congress and is accompanied by his private secretary, Subhas Chandra Bose. Subhas has recently returned from Britain after resigning as an officer of the coveted Indian Civil Service. He is a tall man—about the same age as Anand—with soft features. His round eyeglasses give him a scholarly air. Rumour is that he is a skilled orator and a champion for aggressive nationalism. But the person who captivates Anand's attention is a slim figure standing on stage with ten or twelve other young women. Singing the inspirational ode to the motherland—Bande Mataram—is Sati Sen.

Sati is an art student at Gurudev Rabindranath Tagore's Visva-Bharati university in Santiniketan. They meet for tea at the house of a common acquaintance and discover many mutual interests, the foremost being a love for India. In a few days, the Congress party will splinter with irreconcilable divisions between the supporters of Gandhi and those seeking greater change. Anand, too, is restless. He wishes to travel the world, to do more for India than court arrest. But for the moment, he is certain of two things: first, that he will dedicate his life to India's freedom, and second, he will marry Sati Sen—if she will wait for him.

Anand attempts to travel to the United States to join the revolutionaries of the Ghadar Party. However, the British government intercepts his letters and rejects his passport application. Following the recommendation of an acquaintance, he applies for a passport to Japan, hoping to get it extended to the United States from Tokyo in the future. His passport application is successful.

***

Towards the end of March 1923, Anand arrives in his ancestral village near Bhagalpur, two hundred and fifty kilometres east of Patna. He is here to say goodbye to his parents and his large extended family. His father's expression is grim, and his grandmother is weeping silently. He is the eldest son, and instead of supporting his family, he is leaving for an indefinite period. With a stoic smile, his mother hands him a tin of ghee, fine rice and two hundred rupees in cash. It is a gift he finds difficult to accept; the family is always short of funds. Take it, she urges, explaining that she bought the goods by pawning her ornaments. The men of the family escort Anand to Nathnagar railway station. He rushes past the noisy steam locomotive and boards a third-class carriage. Thus begins his journey east.

Unknown to all but one, he gets off at Bolpur station, a few hours short of Calcutta. In his breast pocket is a letter from Sati Sen. Learning of his imminent departure, Sati urges him to visit Santiniketan. The excuse is a letter of introduction by one of her professors, W.W. Pearson, to his Japanese friend, Mr Okumura. Anand knows no one in Japan and concedes that the letter will be exceedingly useful. But, in his heart, he knows he makes the journey not for the letter but for Sati.

***

Anand returns to India in 1927. He marries Sati, and she is eager to accompany him to Japan. They board the *SS Tilawa*, a large cargo and passenger ship owned by the British India Steam Navigation Company. The ship halts in Singapore for a week. Anand, travelling under the guise of a merchant, is invited to give a speech at the Indian Chamber of Commerce. His speech quickly turns into an impassioned diatribe against the 'white oppressor that has bled India'. The applause in the auditorium is thunderous. The next morning, he is escorted to the Intelligence Branch of the police commissioner's office and interrogated. Sati is not surprised—she knows Singapore is a British colony. And she knows Anand, like herself, is married to the ideal of freedom.

Over the next few years, the Sahays settle into a small two-storeyed wooden home on the outskirts of Kobe. In quick succession, they have three daughters and a son. Throughout their years in Japan, Anand and Sati do everything to support the Indian freedom struggle. Anand starts a branch of the Indian National Congress in Kobe and becomes its president. Together, they publish a monthly magazine called the *Voice of India*, shrewdly published in Japanese and English, promoting the message of Indian nationalism among Japanese readers eager to practise their English. Through their resourcefulness and contacts with Indian merchants and the Japanese intelligentsia, they gather funds to open India Lodge, a shelter for young students, merchants, and even nationalists—filling a void that perhaps Anand felt when he first set foot on Japanese soil. Over the next decade, he travels across East Asia and establishes several outposts of the Indian Independence League. He works with revolutionaries like Rash Behari Bose—wanted by the British police since 1912 for a failed assassination attempt on the then viceroy, Lord Hardinge—and Raja Mahendra Pratap, the president of the first Provisional Government of India (in Exile).

It is 1938, and Asha, the writer of this memoir, turns ten. Celebrations are muted since her father is often travelling. Subhas Chandra Bose, the young leader whom Anand and Sati met in Gaya in 1922, is elected as the president of the Indian National Congress. His admirers call him Netaji, or leader, and Bose—unlike Gandhi—is fire. Freedom, he says, can only be achieved with violence. Again, there is an irreconcilable rift in the Indian National Congress, and, after lengthy disagreements with

Gandhi, Bose, who had been re-elected president of the Congress in 1939, resigns.

Anand and Sati have been supporters of the Indian National Congress for decades; however, they concur with Bose's ideology. He is the leader the movement needs. Via secret channels, they let him know that East Asia is primed for a leader like him. In 1941, Bose makes a daring escape from Calcutta to Germany via Kabul, Moscow and Rome. Outmanoeuvring British intelligence, he seeks the assistance of Nazi Germany to free India, but support is not forthcoming. At the height of the Second World War, Netaji makes a hazardous journey from Germany to Japan in a German U-boat. He travels along the tip of Africa, surfacing briefly near Madagascar to transfer to a Japanese submarine, and arrives in Tokyo in June 1943.

Asha, fifteen years old, leans against a cold concrete pillar in the lobby of Imperial Hotel (or Teikoku Hotel to give its Japanese name). She hums a Bengali song under her breath while tracing the intricate bas-relief work with a finger. She notices her sister, Tulu, chatting fervently a little distance away. Her father is not visible, but her mother has a fiery look in her eyes. Asha impatiently observes the gathering. She has heard many stories about Netaji from her parents: about his life, his heroism, his love for India. In her eyes, he breathes with the gods.

She hears a stir. As she looks up, Netaji Subhas Chandra Bose swiftly descends to the gallery. Asha steps forward. It is a moment that will change the trajectory of her life forever.

THE SAHAY FAMILY

Bharati Sahay (Asha). Lieutenant, Rani of Jhansi Regiment, Indian National Army.

Anand Mohan Sahay (Papa), Asha's father. Freedom fighter and a revolutionary in Japan since 1923; later, a part of the cabinet of the Azad Hind Government.[2]

Sati Sen Sahay (Ma or Mama-san), Asha's mother.

Satyadev Sahay (Satya Kaka), Asha's uncle. Director, Intelligence Bureau, Indian National Army.

Riziya Sahay (Tulu), Asha's sister, younger by two years.

Sumona Sahay (Baby), Asha's other sister, younger by four years.

Ashok Sahay, Asha's brother, younger by eight years.

ASHA-SAN'S JOURNEY ACROSS ASIA

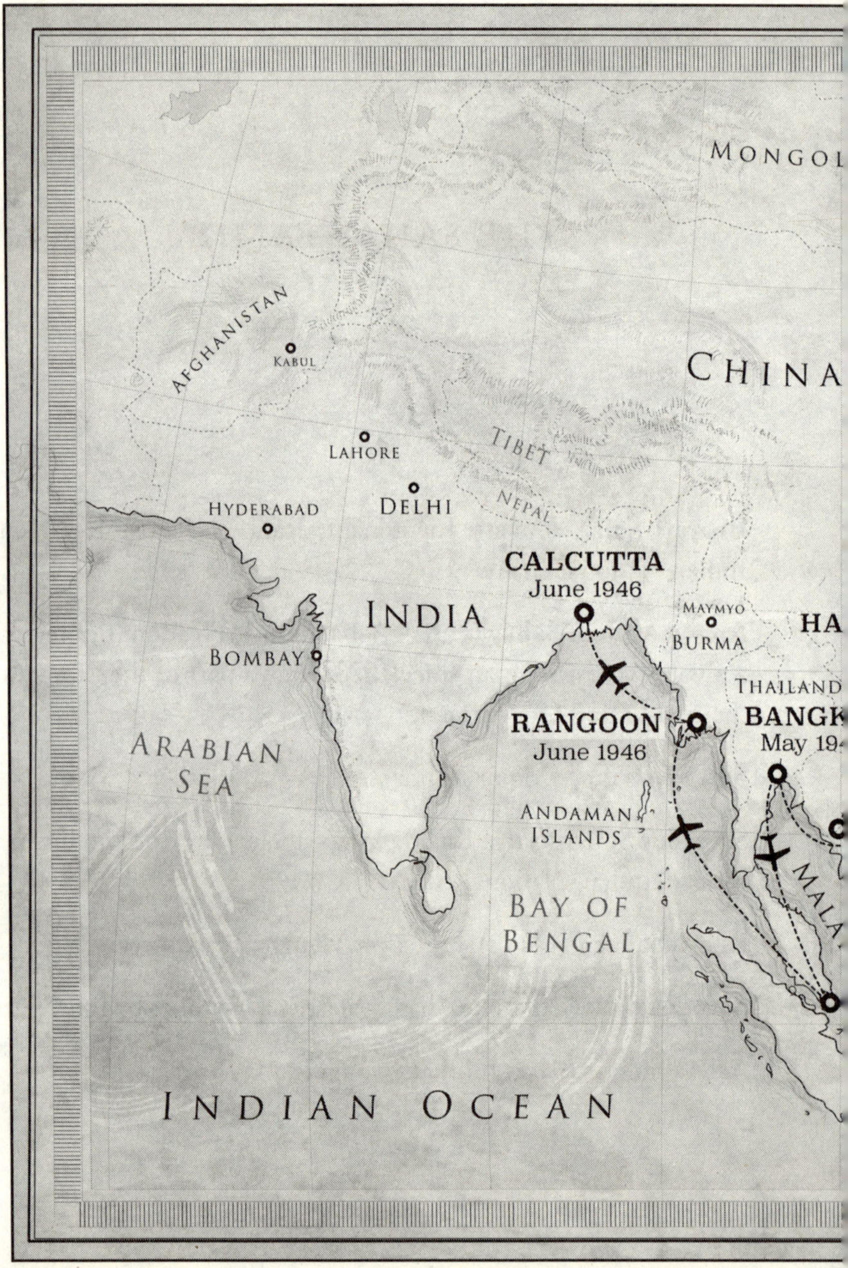

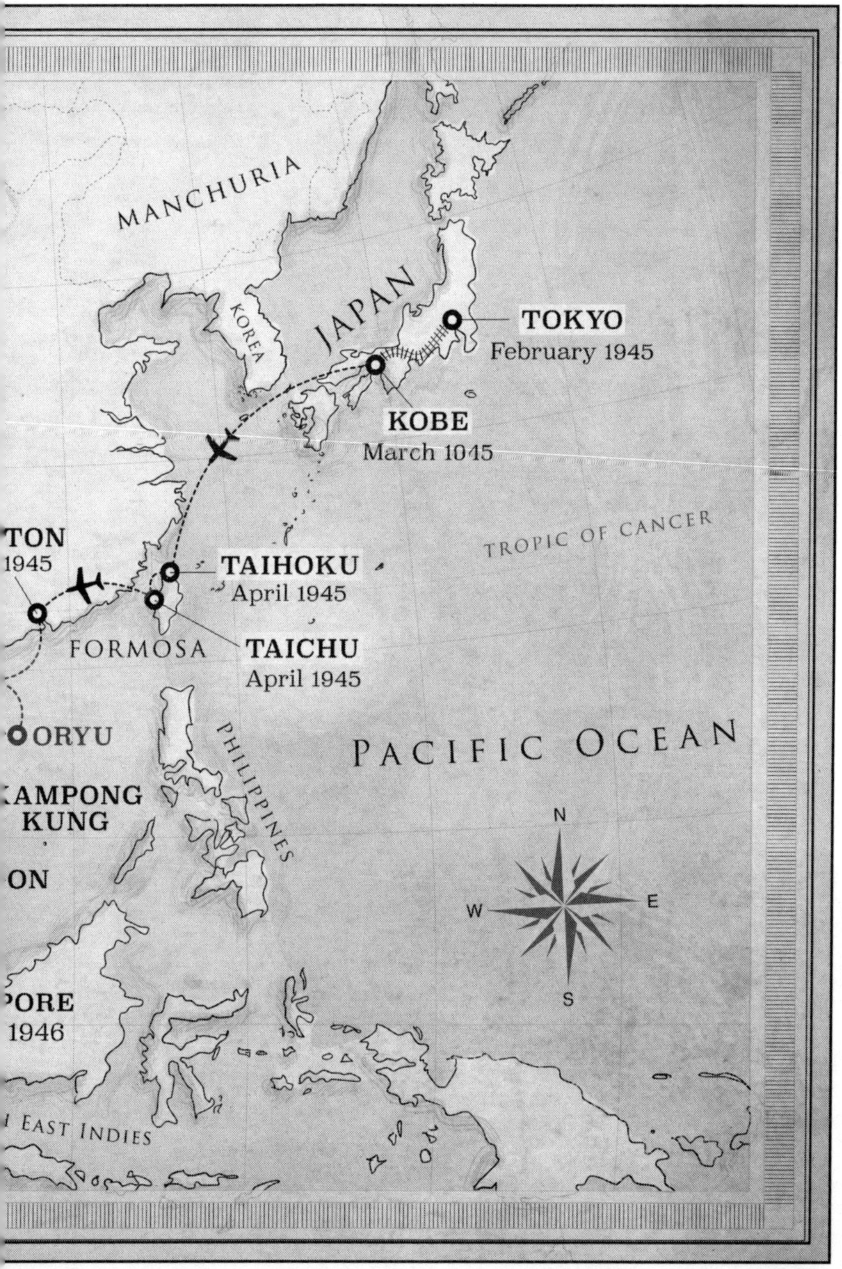

MANCHURIA
KOREA
JAPAN
TOKYO
February 1945
KOBE
March 1045
TON
1945
TAIHOKU
April 1945
FORMOSA
TAICHU
April 1945
TROPIC OF CANCER
ORYU
PHILIPPINES
PACIFIC OCEAN
AMPONG
KUNG
ON
N
W
E
S
PORE
1946
EAST INDIES

Part One

June 1943

Another day passes without a letter from Papa. It is possible that the plane carrying his letter has crashed into the depths of the ocean, unknown to us. April has gone and so has May; we received one letter in March, but, since then, nothing. Rama Murti Kaka, the head of the Indian Independence League (IIL) in Tokyo, shares news from the south: the Indians who had left from Kobe and Tokyo are busy setting up base for the Indian National Army (INA) in Bangkok and Shonan. Following Japan's stormy invasion, Singapore has been renamed Shonan, meaning 'Light of the South', and they say it is only a matter of time before Burma gains freedom.

Papa and Rash Behari Bose met some Japanese officers several months ago and convinced them that Japan and India had to fight together against colonization. As a consequence, the Japanese have freed hundreds of imprisoned Indian soldiers of the British Army under the condition that they join the INA. The soldiers of the INA will fight alongside the Japanese in Burma. Together means no hierarchy, no inferiority.

In his last letter, Papa wrote that we must take delight in our obligations and instructed us to take care of Ma to the best of our abilities. Her body is not as strong as it used to be. Let's see when his next letter arrives. Satya Kaka is on tour, sometimes in Yokohama, sometimes in Kobe.

Sunday, 13 June 1943

Satya Kaka returns from Kobe. We make plans of going to Yokohama with him for an excursion. But as soon as we reach Tokyo station, we spot a newspaper. Printed in bold letters: 'Subhas Bose Arrives on Submarine.' We immediately return home.

Hearing the news, Ma becomes ecstatic. She turns to Kaka and says: 'Satto, let's go to Imperial Hotel immediately.'[3]

'Arre, Bhauji, at this time? Let's wait till the morning.'

Ma relents, but her excitement is contagious and spreads among us. We spend the night talking about Netaji.

Monday, 14 June 1943

Warm rays of hope envelope us this morning, dissipating the numbness of the previous months. We reach Imperial Hotel at about ten in the morning. While we are waiting in the gallery, we hear a stir. I look up and see Netaji Subhas Chandra Bose descending the stairs with his personal secretary, Abid Hasan. Ma greets him by touching his feet and we follow her example.

Netaji says: 'What is this, Sati? What have you taught the children? Do we still have to bow our heads in front of others? And touch their feet, too? Is slavery still around?'

Ma shrivels.

Netaji asks in a softer tone: 'Is everything alright? You aren't facing any difficulties with money, are you?'

As if Ma is one to admit defeat; there is no chance she will share her sufferings.

Standing up straight, she says: 'Everything is fine.' She then turns to Satya Kaka and introduces him to Netaji, who immediately pulls him closer and proceeds to embrace him.

'Subhas Da, please take him as well,' Ma says.

Netaji consents. Who would not be excited to find a warrior like Satya Kaka? I look towards my young uncle, and see his face glowing with happiness and pride. He will now live as a shadow of Netaji.

Kaka secretly came to Japan from India when he was nineteen years old.[4] He began living with us, assisting Ma and Papa in all manners. While Papa may have been his mentor, Ma was his first guide—it is from her he received the affection and consciousness that made him a patriot. For us, he quickly became an ideal; we both revered and adored him.

Kaka enjoys drawing, even though his art often causes us to break into peals of laughter. On one occasion, he was drawing a girl with a long nose, enormous eyes, wide lips and long hair, and we burst out laughing. Kaka acted shocked and said: 'Arre, I've drawn something so beautiful and you all are laughing!' We learnt freehand in school, and to watch him measure and draw made us uncomfortable.

Once, a long time ago, Tulu was wrestling with Kaka. Ma observed them for a while, a curious expression on her face. She then laughed and said: 'Satto, if you go to Purani Sarai and wrestle with a girl, then I'll understand.'[5]

In school, our classmates teased us about Kaka, calling him 'a burnt omelette' or as 'black as coal'. They asked us if he permed his hair. While we felt irritated, we said nothing because he did have curly hair. When we returned home, we grumbled to Kaka. But he was not one to complain, nor did he ever lack friends.

He retorted by saying: 'Yes, it is because I am dark that I am surrounded by crowds of friends.'

I must confess I did not care much for most of his friends; they made us feel Kaka belonged to them and not to us. I used to be most irritated by Tamura-san, who teased me a lot. But I really liked Midori One-san.

Well, Kaka now belongs to no one but Netaji.

We return home from Imperial Hotel. We have been invited to a tea party tomorrow. Day and night, we speak only of Netaji, the worshipper of Ranachandika—an avatar of the Goddess Durga—and Mother India. What we know of him is only through Ma's words. For us, he is like the heroes we read about in books. We cannot greet him with folded hands or bent heads. Neither is it possible to shy away our eyes because of his shimmering charm; he is a divine spectre who brings clarity and consciousness on sight. We stand tall, arms raised in victory, head high, fists balled with strength. Ma is Indian, and she has not forgotten the culture of India, and that is why she told us to touch Netaji's feet. She told us to touch our venerable Netaji's feet and not the feet of a non-entity. If any enemy faces her, Ma will undoubtedly take the form of Kali.

The stories of Indian gods and goddesses are very interesting. I wish I could sit and listen to endless tales about them. Japan considers India to be Tenjiku, or the path to heaven. The people of Japan believe India to be a holy land and they hold Indian culture in high esteem.

A few days ago, Netaji met the prime minister of Japan, General Tojo, and had open and frank discussions with him. General Tojo welcomed Netaji and promised him that the Japanese government would always support the Indian freedom struggle. Netaji's courage and personality duly impressed him.

Tuesday, 15 June 1943

Today, many Indian expatriates gather at the tea party at Imperial Hotel. There are only Indians at the party, not a single Japanese person. Therefore, we must speak in Hindustani; we do not dare speak in English or Japanese.[6]

Tulu and I stand by Ma, repeatedly pestering her. Finally, she relents and agrees to speak to Netaji on our behalf. She will ask him to take us to Bangkok to admit us into the Rani of Jhansi Regiment (RJR).

Netaji, smiling softly, says: 'Will these two be able to fight in a war? So delicate.'

I feel as though someone has lit a fire within me. Glowing with passion and anger, I interrupt them in a mixture of broken Hindi and Bengali: 'We can fight. We can also die for our country.'

How can I stay silent when someone calls me weak and helpless, even if that person is Netaji himself?

Netaji smiles again when he hears my determined tone. How bizarre! A slight laugh on the face of a man with such a solemn personality makes him suddenly seem humble, almost lovable, as though the spring sun has emerged from behind clouds.

He says to Ma: 'Sati, these girls of yours may look meek, but they are made of stone.'

Ma looks at us fondly and says: 'Now, don't get excited.'

Netaji then turns to us. 'We will take you when your father returns to Japan. At least one of you. I think you can go, Asha. Tulu can remain with Ma; she is still young.'

I start dancing, not noticing Tulu's face shrivelling with disappointment.

After the tea party, we return home. Tulu is silent. She isn't talking to anyone. She goes to her bed and slips under a blanket. I can understand that she is feeling immensely sad; Netaji has chosen me and not her. I also realize the war will separate us for the first time and the chances of a reunion are slim. For an instant I feel like going to call her, but I let her be. Being brought up in a stern environment has taught me that showing affection is a source of embarrassment. Sometimes, in other homes, I notice how much love parents shower on their children. It's very different in our home, but our firm upbringing is fine for me. Without the rebukes of Ma, the house would seem lifeless.

Ma scolds Tulu gently. 'There's no need to be so sad. Asha is older; she will go first and then you can follow her.'

Tulu says: 'Yes, all the good things happen to Asha, and I am left here alone.' She bursts into tears. She becomes alright a little while later and eats dinner with us before falling asleep.

Wednesday, 16 June 1943

Today, Ma is making Bengali food. God knows for how long she has stashed away the ingredients—moong dal and Indian masalas; things we don't like at all.

Tulu and I take the food to Imperial Hotel. Netaji is busy with some work, and so Hasan Kaka and Habib Kaka meet us. Looking at the food, they swell with happiness. Hasan Kaka is unnecessarily affectionate. He looks at us and laughs in such a manner that one would think we are his daughters. He doesn't understand that affection is not expressed openly in Japan. He's grown his beard like a saint, a slip of a smile visible between all that hair. He beckons us over. I have no desire to go, but proceed only because he is Papa's friend.

When I tell Ma about my urge to pull his beard she explains: 'Looking at you, he must be remembering his daughters; he's been away from his family for many years. India does not lack patriots who have given up everything for the country. You have grown up here in Japan knowing freedom, and that's why you won't know the true meaning of subordination. Millions of Indians have endured two hundred years of British atrocities. India is a country of unknown heroes who wear the red cloth of sacrifice, willing to face all kinds of dangers.

'Remember Pratap Kaka (Raja Mahendra Pratap)? The British cruelly murdered his family because he believed in independence and self-rule. He did not cow down, but continued to sing "*Bande Mataram*". Pratap Kaka escaped to Japan, and spread the religion of world love and brotherhood. Rash Behari Bose was a similar yogi, who found meaning by dedicating his life to Mother India. Papa, Kaka and I have chosen a life in which serving the nation will always be our dharma and our karma—our religion and our duty. Anyway, you are of the age where all roads lead to India; and for its freedom, you will fight to your last breath.'

All four of us keep looking at Ma; she is truly a goddess. When she was sixteen years old, the British arrested my grandmother, Didima, sister of Deshbandhu Chittaranjan Das, along with my grand-aunt, Basanti Devi, wife of Deshbandhu. Familial relationships in those days were pointless; there were only two relationships—deshpremi (a patriot) and deshdrohi (a traitor)—that mattered. Hearing about the journey of the patriots to jail, volunteer groups gathered and shouted 'Bande Mataram' on the roads of Calcutta. Everyone, including Ma, walked towards Presidency Jail. Girls in white sarees with red borders, walking barefoot, waving the tricolour. How many Ranis of Jhansi walked free that day! Suddenly, a whistle blew and the police surrounded them. They were thrashed with lathi sticks. The officers giving the orders were British, but those who rained the blows were Indian. A few of them even said to Ma: 'Sister, forgive me; I am on duty.'

Damn those who consider the orders of the enemy to be their duty. Damn them for raising their hands on their own sisters.

Saturday, 19 June 1943

Netaji speaks at a press conference at Imperial Hotel today. 'We must immediately transform civil disobedience into a strong struggle for independence. Only when Indians complete a trial by fire on a large scale will they be entitled to their independence.'

Some important words Netaji says on the occasion: 'India will be free and before long. And, Free India will throw open the prison gate, so that her worthy sons may step out of the darkness of the prison cells into the light of freedom, joy and self-fulfilment. Indian freedom must, however, be won with Indian blood…'

Sunday, 27 June 1943

Netaji is leaving Tokyo today. He tells me that when Papa returns to Japan in two or three months, I should join him and head to the RJR training camp in Bangkok.

Netaji will return to the battlefield, leaving an indelible mark not only on the Indians but also on the Japanese who have crossed his path. Hitler visited Japan and so did Mussolini; Sukarno and Pibul Songgram (Phibunsongkhram) also came, but no one left such an impact on the citizens of Japan as Netaji. They feared some leaders, were curious about others, but Netaji alone had the ability to successfully reach the hearts of the Japanese. He has the unusual ability of hypnotizing his audience. Hearing him speak once makes people restless to join him in the battlefield—such are the feelings of excitement and strength he inspires. The same thing happened to me. After meeting him, I, too, had the intense urge to do something for my motherland. Thoughts of hunger disappeared; we found new hope, and life suddenly became more bearable.

We are facing difficulties at every step, but in this, there is happiness, not sadness. The state of war means being fine and not fine at the same time. Victory is visible. But in the Pacific Ocean, there is no peace; terror shadows us.

Saturday, 10 July 1943

The situation of the war turns grimmer by the day. There are no young men left in any homes in Japan. They are either on the battlefield or have already attained martyrdom. We are continuously seeing American planes, and thousands are dying every day. Destruction dances naked before our eyes. By the orders of the Japanese government, the young and the elderly are being transferred to remote villages. Baby and Ashok have been evacuated to the hills of Niigata-ken in the north, along with their schoolmates.[7] Baby has become Ashok's guardian; in any case, she is the only one who keeps him in check.

With the two of them gone, our home feels empty, but there is less to worry about: they no longer have to face the flames of bombs or hunger. Ma has arranged for Tulu and me to stay in a hostel called Peony House because, over there, at least as per rules, meals are given. We can keep in good health and study without discomfort. The superintendent is a gentle and sophisticated lady belonging to the Japanese imperial family. She reminds me of a cool autumn breeze. I want to ask Ma what will happen to her? How will she stay alone? But the fear of being reprimanded keeps me silent. God has given her so much strength that she can stay alone in any condition, despite her arthritis. That's why Papa and Kaka have placed everything on Ma's shoulders and left.

Papa's letter arrives. We don't know where it has come from. It's possible that he is currently in the jungles near Rangoon. Reading it, Ma's face lights up.

'Papa is coming, na?' I ask.

'Keep quiet. Let me read it first,' she says curtly. 'Here, take your letter.' She passes an envelope that contains a letter for both Tulu and me. I don't have the courage to ask her anything else. Swallowing my questions, we wait for Papa's arrival.

Tuesday, 10 August 1943

Writing daily in my diary feels like a splendid exercise. A passion has become a habit. But what kind of diary is this, forever filled with war, hunger, doubt and despair? Ma has called us home from the hostel, but ever since we have returned there have been no letters from Papa. We are doing our duties mechanically; we have given up trying to find solutions to our problems.

From the bank, we receive money to buy ration and pay the doctor's fees; we do not get a single extra yen. Anyway, what would we do with money when the markets are in a shambles? From the ration shop, we get enough to eat, even if it is only pumpkin day after day. We've been eating boiled pumpkin for the last three months. We've heard we'll get potatoes next time. We often get to hear things like this—the war is about to end; the rations will increase; everything will be available in the market once again; Japan will defeat the Yankee forces, and so on. Yet, no one remains under the spell of these rumours. We are here today, we exist in this moment; tomorrow, a bomb may fall on our roof and we may die; then what is the point of being concerned with the black market and other comforting disinformation? Life and death have become subjects we discuss casually. I have a desire to live so that I can enlist in Netaji's army and serve the nation.

Coincidentally, there was an incident today.

It began when Tsutomu, a boy who lives in our neighbourhood, teased me this morning: 'Today you left your hostel for your mother. What will happen tomorrow when you go to your in-law's house?'

'Oh, you,' I said heatedly. 'You won't even have in-laws. Which girl will want to marry someone who hesitates to go to war? You're eighteen years old now and you're still sitting at home. You haven't even finished military school; if I were you, I would die of shame.'

I said it sarcastically, but there was enough substance in the joke to reveal an uncomfortable truth.

At around 5 p.m., Tsutomu's sister comes running up to us and says breathlessly: Sati-san, Asha-san, come quickly! Where is the spade? Bring it and come quickly, Asha-san. Tsutomu … in the mud…'

She runs back with madness in her step. I pick up the spade and begin running behind her. Ma follows us. Tsutomu was trying to widen the trench from the inside. The roof of the trench collapsed and all the earth above fell on his head. He is still buried somewhere within. We quickly begin removing the earth. Gradually, we can see his head. I, along with many others, start removing the surrounding mud. Soon, we can see his body and we pull him out. He is unconscious and his face has turned blue. We brush away the mud and sprinkle water on his face. Tulu has gone to fetch the doctor, but neither have arrived.

Half an hour later, Tsutomu's lips flutter. Ma and Tsutomu's mother begin massaging his hands and feet. We put two–three drops of water in his mouth, and a few moments later, we hear a groan. His eyes open, pupils spinning wildly, and then close again. When his eyes reopen, he starts searching for someone and the Japanese word for 'mother'—kaachan—comes to his lips.

Together, we take him home. Tsutomu's mother, who, till that moment, was working frantically but mechanically, sees that her son is fine. She crumples to the floor and collapses in tears. A few minutes later, she gets up and goes to the shrine of her ancestors. They are kept in a separate room along with the throne of the sun goddess, the ancestor of the Japanese emperor. We assume she is thanking her ancestors, head bowed, filled with gratitude that her son has survived. She returns to the room half an hour later with a tray in her hands containing steaming balls of rice.

Etiquette prevents us from jumping with joy, but we cannot stop our mouths from watering.

Ma says: 'But what are you doing? There is no rice available and you are distributing it so freely?'

Tsutomu's mother replies: 'Today, I have made all the rice I had and am giving it to you because my eyes have been opened. I am happy because Tsutomu has been given a new birth, which he is going to make meaningful. I was selfish, so I always kept him near me; I even put him in the ineligible category. But today, I realize that life and death are not in our hands. So what will I do keeping this rice? Who knows what will happen—today my storeroom has rice and tomorrow it will turn to ashes. Now, please start eating.'

We eat till the tray is empty. Satiated and joyful, we bid everyone farewell. I spot Tsutomu as I am leaving.

He says in a faint voice: 'Asha-san, our in-laws are waiting for us in heaven. We will find them once we achieve martyrdom, isn't it?'

'Of course,' I say softly and ask him to go to sleep.

The evening slips by us and night falls. Like all nights, Mosquitoes—the American fighter planes—hover over us as unwanted guests. Some bombs fall here, some there.

Wednesday, 25 August 1943

After many days, we finally receive a letter from Papa. An officer of the Hikari Kikan—the Japanese organization liaising with the Indian National Army—arrives at our place unannounced.[8] He gives us news of Papa's well-being and hands over an envelope to Ma. We learn from him that tremendous efforts are being made to establish the Azad Hind Government and the INA in Shonan. The Army's 1st Guerrilla Division—the Subhas Regiment—is ready. Its commander will be Shah Nawaz Khan. The officer's eyes shimmer as he describes Subhas Chandra Bose's patriotism. The Japanese often think of Indians—Indojin—with negative sentiments—slaves, scoundrels, black people—but today, they revere all Indians because of the honour one Indian has brought to the country on the global altar.

We learn from Ma's letter that Papa has gone on a tour to China with Netaji and will soon head from Bangkok to Burma. After this, there is hope that he will come to Japan.

After reading Papa's letter, we all feel inspired again.

At night, Ma tells us the story of Rani of Jhansi, Rani Lakshmi Bai, the same queen after whom our 'Rani of Jhansi Regiment' has been named. We practise some nationalistic songs—qaumi geet—and fall asleep. Later at night, American bombers begin attacking and we have to rise. We've been in the trench for an hour.

Friday, 10 September 1943

Today is Papa's birthday. Ma asked Rama Murti Kaka to send a telegram to Bangkok congratulating Papa. Then she cancelled her request; now is not the time to celebrate birthdays. Ma makes a dessert with potatoes and milk and we ravenously attack it.

The gathering of the tonarigumi is taking place at our home in a few hours. 'Tonarigumi' means a neighbourhood association. During this period of war, similar associations have been created all over Japan by the government—usually limited to ten homes in one group. The aim is not only for women to protect and organize their homes but those of the entire neighbourhood. In Japan, one difficulty faced all over the country is the absence of men: all men aged twenty to forty have gone to the southern

Asian front to fight the enemy. Only women, children, and the elderly remain at home.

Each member of the tonarigumi is assigned a duty to help the neighbourhood. For example, every six weeks, a member collects rations for the group. Whatever ration is procured is distributed in these gatherings. Be it one fish or one watermelon, it is divided based on the number of members in each family. The homes with children get the centre portion of the fish, the homes with just the elderly get the head, and the homes with only women get a section of the tail. Sometimes a box of cigarettes, sometimes a bar of chocolate (only once in three months, divided among all the children). That's why I gave the cigarettes to Ojiisan, the grandpa who lives in our neighbourhood. In those homes, where there is no one but the elderly or the very young, the people of the neighbourhood take care of them, too. Mothers send their children into their homes to clean and do other housework.

Young girls and women complete their duties before heading to work or going to school or college. Even in the evening, adolescent girls try to take care of the elderly or the sick. If, in any group, a young man is about to head off to war, the entire tonarigumi makes home food, and gathers to see him off at the railway station, a white-and-crimson-red Hinomaru flag (the name of the Japanese national flag, meaning 'circle of the sun') in hand. And if a youth of any home attains martyrdom, the neighbourhood group accompanies the family to bring home his ashes.

The group elects the president, usually the woman who gives the best instructions for the welfare of the neighbourhood. It is also an opportunity to solve any discord among the women of the neighbourhood. We discuss societal matters, educational matters and so on, in this small gathering.

Today, Ma has also invited Ojiisan. Everyone brings their own cushions. Sitting on the floor is a custom in Japan, and each home has a set of small cushions, for both themselves and guests. After everyone gathers, Ma offers Japanese tea on a tray, and says: 'It is good that you all brought your cushions; in these times of difficulty, who knows where we would have got more cushions from.'

One woman says: 'Sahay-san, tell us something about the women of India?'

Ma replies: 'There is a lot to say, but at the moment, we have to deal with our present circumstances, too, so I will tell you briefly. We have been enduring British atrocities for hundreds of years. The most important thing is that the Indian woman has always held her head high. Many brave women have fought and sacrificed their lives. They have jumped into fires to forever protect themselves. Yes, it's true that in society, there are false egos, superstitions and useless customs. But women are striding ahead by serving the nation, serving society. Women sit at home and spin cotton from wheels to become self-sufficient; they teach those of the backward classes; they are taking part in efforts to make the country free by hiding patriots and revolutionaries in their homes. They are secretly helping the freedom struggle.

'There are also some women in society who prefer to be stooges of the British. Sometimes, I wish I could show them life in Japan, where people are willing to endure innumerable sufferings for the country. We are living together and sharing everything together. We will strive to make this kind of life in Free India, too.'

Friday, 15 October 1943

An impatient mind will never find peace. We received Papa's letter some time ago; in it he said he was coming home soon. We thought he would come by the end of the week. He did not arrive. We thought he would come within the month, but, instead of him, winter wrapped Tokyo in its arms. In my head, too, cold air buzzes. Is it pointless to seek the wanderers who walk the path of freedom? We become consumed by our daily tasks. In this stagnant life, our only entertainment—airplane dogfights—have also lessened. Now swarms of bombers arrive and bomb Tokyo and other cities, leaving endless graveyards in their wake.

Today, we are late in returning from college. At the bus stand, there is a queue at the shop selling cutlets. Why not, I think, standing with Tulu in the queue. After waiting for half an hour, we receive four cutlets. Soon, the bus also arrives.

While holding onto the handrail, I say: 'It's strange; I feel like I'm in heaven because there's a cutlet in my hand.'

Tulu responds quickly: 'It's natural. We're hungry; we're getting something to eat while we're having fun. What's strange about it?'

When we reach home, Ma is grim. Seeing her in this form makes us fearful; what secrets lay hidden behind her sternness?

She quietly places a fat envelope before us. 'Look. It's come from the Japanese Headquarters.'

Tulu opens the envelope, reads it, and begins laughing. I, too, read the letter. Papa is coming, Papa is coming in one week. He will stay in Tokyo for at least twenty days. Along with Papa, Netaji, Hasan Kaka and some others are also coming. They will take part in the soon-to-be-held Greater East Asia Conference in Tokyo and will hold discussions with the Japanese government. While we are jumping with joy, Ma gently places a cutlet on a plate and pours us some tea.

At night, Ma and Tulu slip into a blanket. I, too, will get in with them. Tonight, Ma will tell us a long story where Papa will undoubtedly be the hero.

Wednesday, 20 October 1943

We are whiling away time waiting for Papa. For some days, Tulu has been looking different. She laughs with us and sings with us, but, in her laughter and in her song, there is a strange hollowness. Whenever there is talk of me going to Bangkok, she becomes anxious. I had thought when the time comes everything would be alright. But clearly, thinking achieves nothing. I am truly worried about how Tulu will live alone. I know I must be fearless, but I can't bear to look at her sad face. Getting admitted to the RJR and erasing myself for Mother India is now my only objective. So, I must not worry about someone else's sadness, be it that of my sister.

I've heard that the Azad Hind Government will be established on 21 October.

Thursday, 21 October 1943

We are hearing great news on Radio Tokyo today: Shonan's Cathay Cinema witnesses the declaration of the establishment of the Azad Hind Government. Netaji Subhas Chandra Bose inaugurates the day with a speech. He says that for the establishment of Azad Hind rule, we not only have the full support of the Indian diaspora but also have received and will continue to receive the help of the soldiers of the British Indian Army. He has complete faith that it will not take us and our brave forces much time to reach India. Now, as soon as we are at the borders of India, British rule will end. There are not many days left before full independence is established in India.

The radio continues: 'After the speech, Netaji takes an oath, his voice clouded with emotion. Following him are the other senior officers of the government, taking their oath one by one.

'In the name of God, I, Subhas Chandra Bose, take the oath that I will live for and die for India's freedom. I will forever be a servant of Mother India. And I will consider serving the brothers and sisters of my country my very first duty. Even after achieving complete independence, I will be ready to maintain this freedom till my last breath. Jai Hind!'[9]

After taking the oath, everyone sings nationalistic songs, followed by Rabindranath Tagore's famous song '*Jana gana mana*' translated into Hindustani.

Shubh sukh chain ki barkha barse,
Bharat bhagya hai jaga.
May the rains of auspiciousness and joy fall,
as India awakens to her destiny.

Then slogans are chanted, followed by thunderous applause. The announcer says that foreigners attending the ceremony look astonished and watch the spectacle with wide eyes. It is an event they will undoubtedly share with their countrymen on their return.

I cannot believe what I am hearing. A single thought enters and leaves my mind like the waves of the sea: are we truly free? Is it really true that we no longer will have to bow our heads in front of someone else? Is it actually possible that we have our own government at last? And an army that has both heroes and heroines?

We are enthralled when we imagine Papa on the same stage, taking the same oath. How magnificent he must be looking in the uniform of the Azad Hind Government.

Sunday, 24 October 1943

Tonight, at five minutes past midnight, the Indian National Army declares war against Britain and America as an independent army. An act that was impossible within our nation has become possible because of the patriots who live beyond its borders. Two halves will unite as one. When we, the patriotic diaspora of India, meet our fellow countrymen at India's borders, no strength in the universe can hinder our progress. Today, the Azad Hind Government receives recognition from many other countries: Japan, Burma, Manchuria, Korea, Germany, Philippines, Nanking, Thailand and Italy send letters of recognition.

Several Japanese newspapers, including *Yomiuri* and *Asahi*, publish news of the Azad Hind Government and Netaji's speech in bold letters. I read the speeches as they appear in the Japanese newspapers aloud to Ma. Is this a speech or virtuous rain? Each sentence feels like the thrust of a sword.

Netaji and the Azad Hind Government do not have to use force to raise funds. There is nothing but love for the nation in the hearts of the Indian diaspora—mostly ordinary people. An elderly man without family stands near Netaji. 'I have given everything,' he says. 'My son, my daughter-in-law, and my wealth. Now please give me and my wife some work to do for the nation.' They immediately receive work in Netaji's camp and begin their new journey.

Sunday, 31 October 1943

Netaji will be with us today. A car will come for us, and we will proudly go to meet our incredible leader.

Whenever Papa returns home, he sees Tulu and steadies himself. Whether it be at an airport or a railway station, Tulu jumps up and wraps herself around him. The same thing happens today. We meet Papa and some others at the gallery of Imperial Hotel. Tulu jumps up and down like a deer, shouting, 'Papa, Papa.' Papa staggers and controls himself. He looks left and right before saying: 'Oof, Tulu, you'll make me fall. You've become so tall, yet you still dangle from me.'

The rest of us say 'Jai Hind!' Ma is behind us. She is staring at Papa with her large, doe-like eyes.

Tulu says: 'Papa, I, too, want to join the Rani of Jhansi Regiment with Asha.'

'Even Asha is not going right now,' responds Papa. 'The next time I go, then we'll see.'

Tulu immediately becomes happy, and I become discouraged. Anyway…

Netaji has given Papa an order: 'Sahay, go home today and be with your children. But tomorrow, be here at 8 a.m. on the dot.'

Papa assents, standing at attention and saluting.

Netaji says to Ma in Bengali: 'Tor kachche kono chool'er tel thaakle, pathiye deesh.' If you have any hair oil, send it across.

Spontaneously Ma, too, stands at attention and says: 'Yes.'

***

The four of us exit the hotel and head to Tokyo Station. On the train, Ma speaks to Papa in furious Bengali. Japanese travellers stare at them, their eyes filled with respect. Someone looks at Papa and whispers in Japanese, 'He's an officer of the Indogun,' and someone else says, 'He is a minister of Chandora-san.' In Japan, people refer to Netaji as Chandora-san and the INA as Indogun. They recognize that these are lions and lionesses who have sworn to free India.

We reach home and eat our dinner. Papa begins singing nationalistic songs and asks us to sing along. But to sing in front of him leaves us quivering. While Papa sometimes loses the melody, he has a very keen sense of rhythm. After singing several songs, we receive permission to sleep. When Papa is home, it feels like we no longer have a worry in the world.

Monday, 1 November 1943

Today Netaji will meet Japanese Prime Minister General Tojo at the Greater East Asia Conference (Dai Toa Kaigi). Papa leaves early in the morning. With him, he takes a small bottle of Jabakusum Hair Oil, which Ma had ordered from Calcutta before the war, and another small glass bottle of eau de cologne for Netaji.

Saturday, 6 November 1943

Today and tomorrow, the Greater East Asia Conference is taking place in front of the Japanese parliament, the National Diet Building. An impressive stage has been set up in front of the steps of the building with large chairs festooned in red, yellow and golden colours. Prime ministers of all friendly nations have arrived.

Japan's General Tojo, Thailand's Prince Wan Waithayakon, Burma's Ba Maw, and so on.[10] Representing India is Netaji. India is here as an observer. Netaji says that he doesn't have the ability to make India join the co-prosperity sphere.

He says: 'So far as India is concerned, our fate is indissolubly linked up with the fate of Nippon and her allies in this war. If our allies were to go down, there will be no hope for India to be free for at least a hundred years. But we know that this time, providence, fate and luck are on our side, and I want to assure Your Excellency and Excellencies that we, the Indian people, having waited all our life for an international crisis of this sort, are determined to make the fullest use of this opportunity for achieving the final emancipation of our country. For India, there is no other path but the path of uncompromising struggle against

British imperialism. Even if it were possible for other nations to think of compromising with England, for the Indian people, at least, it is out of the question. Compromising with Britain means to compromise with slavery, and we are determined not to compromise with slavery any more.

'I, therefore, want to assure Your Excellencies that come what may, no matter how long and hard the struggle may be, no matter what the suffering and the sacrifice involved may prove to be, we are determined to fight to the bitter end, being fully confident of our final victory.'

Japan's PM General Tojo declares Japan will hand over the Andaman and Nicobar Islands, currently under Japanese occupation, to the Azad Hind Government. Netaji has renamed the two islands 'Shaheed' (martyr) and 'Swaraj' (self-rule).

The welcome Netaji and his followers receive from the Japanese government is unparalleled—no other foreign VIP receives a similar welcome. They call Netaji the god of war. He is taken to all important sites in the country, like the Military College, the Airforce Training College, the weapons armoury, and so on. Japanese Emperor Hirohito and his family also extend respectful hospitality to Netaji.

When Papa returns home, he tells us all these stories. The activities in southern Asia are very interesting. We sit together, hear the stories and then sing songs.

But for how long?

Thursday, 18 November 1943

These, these are what you call fleeting moments. It's hard to understand where time goes. Netaji is gone and so is Papa. Who knows when they will return? Today, we sit huddled together with

Ma. After the despair of the evening, the silence of the night tears us apart.

'For the present, I can offer you nothing except hunger, thirst, privation, forced marches and death. But if you follow me in life and in death, as I am confident you will, I shall lead you to victory and freedom. It does not matter who among us will live to see India free. It is enough that India shall be free and that we shall give our all to make her free!'

Netaji said this.

Our stomachs are empty, but our hearts are filled with enthusiasm. Our eyes are turned towards India. We are receiving all our news from the radio and the newspapers. Our Indian National Army's 1st and 2nd Divisions are moving ahead from Burma's capital, Rangoon. After leaving Tokyo, Netaji and his companions—Papa, General Bhonsle, Colonel Kiani, and so on—reached Shonan via Nanking, Shanghai, Manila and Saigon.

Now, there is nothing left to write in this diary other than the news I hear on the radio. Our shimmering eyes wish to rip apart this darkness and stare in another direction. At the moment, our lives have become nothing more than symbols of uncertainty and darkness.

Sunday, 26 December 1943[11]

Netaji, Papa, Bhonsle Sahib and Kiani Sahib have reached the Andaman (Shaheed) and Nicobar (Swaraj) Islands. The mayor of the island handed over Port Blair to Netaji. A few days later, Colonel Loganathan was appointed the chief commissioner of the islands. The people of the islands warmly welcomed Netaji, as did our recently freed countrymen. Netaji and his companions filled their hearts with the holy rain of devotion and faith.

Thursday, 30 December 1943

Rama Murti Kaka's younger brother has arrived. He brings with him grim news—while Japanese forces are slowly moving ahead from Rangoon, the condition of war is terrible. Two battalions of the INA are also moving towards Arakan, but they are facing terrible adversity: there is nothing to eat or drink. Netaji and the ministers of the Azad Hind Government are raising as much funds and as many supplies as possible.

Those soldiers who run away from the INA, or join hands with the enemy, will be sentenced to death.

Saturday, 22 January 1944

Times of war. Cold that melts your bones. To welcome the new year, we hang the tricolour flag on the gate of our home. According to Japanese custom, we decorate the house with pine, bamboo and plum branches. These three branches—named Sho-Chiku-Bai—symbolize immortality, strength and plurality.

Our college exams are also over and I came in the second division. Bombs fell during our exams; we simply took our answer sheets into the trenches and wrote our exams there.

In Burma, the Japanese forces have retreated in the Arakan battle. The INA, too, got quite a jolt because of this. However, they do not hesitate; they continue to move forward towards Imphal. Maymyo is now under the control of the INA. In Rangoon, Netaji held discussions with the Japanese commander, General Kawabe.

He firmly told General Kawabe: 'No division of the Indian National Army will be fragmented. No member of the Indian National Army will be integrated into the Japanese regiments. Yes, the motive of our battles is the same and will remain the same. But the soldiers of our army will not fall under the shadow of Japanese command.'

He continued: 'Our path is expansive. We must forge ahead. We must never turn back and look at the past. Arise, awaken, your motherland is calling you! Chalo Delhi! (Onward to Delhi!)'

Sunday, 23 January 1944

Today is Netaji's birthday. In Burma, much against his wishes, Netaji is weighed in gold. This gold will be kept for the INA. Young Indian men and women in Malaya, Thailand and Burma are establishing a 'Suicide Corps' by signing their names in blood.

Thursday, 3 February 1944

Fierce battles are ongoing in Arakan. Netaji bids farewell to the Subhas Regiment from Rangoon, standing on the platform till the train becomes a speck in the distance. Now our forces will go to Mandalay and from there, onwards to Imphal. Netaji will go to Maymyo with Papa and Colonel Chatterji. Colonel Chatterji has been appointed the chief administrator of Maymyo. Wherever we are victorious, the Azad Hind establishes its administration, according to military law. Netaji's Azad Hind Dal[12] are to follow the military for urgent tasks, such as rehabilitation, providing supplies, and restoration of law and order. The Japanese have full rights to rule the territories won; however, General Tojo has given explicit instructions that the administration will be in the hands of the Azad Hind Government.

A Japanese battalion joins the INA battalion; they are moving towards Chin Hill.

Wednesday, 8 March 1944

A team of seventy members of the Azad Hind Dal were recruited hurriedly for civil administration.

Sunday, 19 March 1944

Japanese troops and INA soldiers crossed into the Indian frontier. Netaji issued a call to the people of India to cooperate; he prepared a proclamation as Supreme Commander.

May–June 1944

Summer is here. We have packed away all our sweaters and coats. Along with the heat, news from Imphal and Burma has dried up. All we know is that they are still fighting.

Sunday, 16 July 1944[13]

Today is Sunday. Tulu and I return home to meet Ma. Two young Indian men are visiting. Ma introduces them as Karmakar Da and Dasan Da. The Azad Hind Government has sent them to Japan along with forty-three other boys to train as pilots.[14] We say, 'Jai Hind,' and they return the salutation. First, we begin speaking in Japanese, and then later our conversation continues in a mixture of Bengali, English and Japanese. We return to the hostel at four in the evening, leaving a pish-pash of vegetables and rice for Ma.

July 1944

Unexpectedly, we receive a letter from Papa via the hands of a Japanese gentleman. He introduces himself as Kato-san from the Hikari Kikan and shares some stories from the Burma Front.

'The Japanese forces cannot move ahead any more,' he says. 'Only Shah Nawaz Sir's Subhas Regiment and Kiani Sir's 1st Division are moving ahead.' Kato-san praises the leadership of the Azad Hind forces and its brave soldiers. We swell with pride and happiness. He continues: 'Netaji regularly visits North Burma from Rangoon with the aid of his aeroplane, gifted to him by the Japanese government. Sahay is with Colonel Chatterji on the battlefield. He is assisting Netaji by sharing inputs from the front.'

In Rangoon, people are still contributing their wealth and property, and are impatient to hear news of victory. The proprietor of Zeyawaddy Sugar Factory, Parmanandji, has handed over his entire factory to Netaji. Netaji considers this area as a portion of Free India, and all profits of the factory are kept in the treasury of the Azad Hind Government. This has been very helpful for the provisional government, which incurs a monthly expense of about two lakh rupees for the Indian National Army alone. The Indian women of Rangoon have also handed over whatever remaining jewellery they had to Netaji.

Kato-san becomes emotional while speaking. How he must love India. People say that the Japanese government is selfish and that they are doing everything for their own benefit. In my opinion, the Japanese can't be like this. They desire the betterment of Asia; they want unity in Asia. Anyway, now is a time of war. Even the walls have ears. It is better to remain silent. If you want to talk secretively in Japan, you have to leave all the doors and windows open to ensure no one is standing nearby in disguise and eavesdropping.

August–September 1944

The Battle of Imphal ends. An unsuccessful end! The rains came lashing in, halting the progress of our forces, who were attempting to cross the mountainous valleys. Our soldiers faced intolerable misery—hunger, thirst and then death. Because of the rains, transport with the outside world had been cut off and so had the flow of information. The valleys of Imphal were littered with Indian and Japanese corpses.

This unimaginable news somehow reached Rangoon and Netaji's vast heart was tumultuous with grief. He immediately directed all his energies to save the afflicted soldiers. He began marching towards Imphal with his trusted companions. Because of the rains, it was difficult for the soldiers to return. Despite that, they somehow managed to exit the valley and march in a southerly direction. Netaji not only inspected the camps of the INA, but also entered the Japanese cantonment and encouraged the Japanese soldiers. With glimmering eyes, the soldiers of both countries experienced the impact of his personality and tolerance. Rays of hope exploded. Everyone was sad; angry, even. But after hearing what Netaji had to say, they felt inspired and at peace.

He said: 'So what if the rains have taken the side of the enemy? The dry season will come again and soon we will go from Imphal to Manipur.'

Shaheed Diwas, or Martyr's Day, was celebrated on 21 September. In commemoration, Netaji bestowed the status of Sevak-e-Hind and other heroic titles on the martyrs.

We still have no news of Papa.

October–November 1944[15]

On the invitation of Japan's new prime minister, General Koiso, Netaji, Chatterji Sahib and Kiani Sahib arrive in Tokyo. According to an agreement, there will be diplomatic relationships between the Azad Hind Government and the Japanese government. A Japanese ambassador has been appointed, and the independence of the INA has been determined—meaning there will be no relationship with Japanese military laws. Other matters have also been discussed. To solve any financial issues, it has been decided that the INA will take its requirements directly to the Army Supply Division. According to the terms decided, the costs will be borne by the Azad Hind Government. This way there will be no need to seek assistance from the Hikari Kikan.[16] The Japanese government and the Azad Hind Government will have a system of ambassadors to exchange information.

I reach Tokyo University with Tulu and Ma. Netaji will be giving a speech here shortly.

I learn a lot from Netaji's words. He says: 'I have always been a follower of Mahatma Gandhi. However, I disagree with his concept of satyagraha, or non-violent resistance. I have and will continue to forever worship his other thoughts, but I will always consider the security of our country as my duty. Only when the country becomes strong can we look at finding solutions to other problems.'

November–December 1944

The situation of the war is bad. In Burma, it is the quiet before the storm. There is unrest in the Pacific Ocean, and much despair and destruction. Earlier in the year, the Azad Hind Government had appointed a commissioner to the Andaman Islands. But because of the arbitrariness of the Japanese army officers, the islanders are unhappy and anxious. The Japanese government's infinite devotion and sympathy seems to be received only by the Azad Hind Government; the local Japanese authorities trouble the people of the islands.

Netaji has gone from Japan to Malaya to begin preparations for a renewed attack. But the defeat in Imphal has left people discouraged. He finds it difficult to inspire the masses. Even then, about three lakh ticals (Siamese currency) has been collected in Bangkok.

We are now hearing detailed stories of the 1944 monsoon rains, the heavy floods in the Irrawaddy and Chindwin rivers. The Indian National Army lost over five hundred soldiers in the thick jungles because of diseases such as malaria and typhoid. Thousands more achieved martyrdom while facing the enemy. Papa, Netaji and some other colleagues were together in Manipur.[17] There was no scope for the import of supplies. They were waiting for days to pass, dependent on tinned food to survive.

Papa composed a nationalistic song while stranded in the jungles. He wished to increase the enthusiasm of the Azad Hind soldiers and wanted to urge the Indian soldiers of the British Army to switch allegiances. The song, written in Hindustani, was relayed over the hills of Manipur by loudspeaker. This is that song:

Soldiers of India, be brave,
forget your mistakes,
fight for your own,
forget fights between one another.

We are your brothers
and you are ours,
come, brothers, let's join together,
and leave this oppression.

After freeing our country,
we will become one.
Forget the claims of the enemy,

raise India's tricoloured flag,
and be the one to say Jai Hind.

Be brave, soldiers of India,
leave the enemy's oppression,
come join us,
together we will go to Delhi
and free India.

January 1945

The new year arrives bringing with it fresh enthusiasm and vitality. From Papa's letters, we gather he will return to Japan within a month. But from what we read of the war in the newspapers, we know hoping for his return is pointless. Rama Murti Kaka tells us that Netaji has given the commanders of the INA instructions to keep the spirits of their soldiers high—those who hesitate on the battlefield should return. It is better to return than show one's back to the enemy.

A division of the INA is closing in on the border. They are trying to cross the Irrawaddy and Kaladan rivers. Colonel Dhillon is the commander of the Guerrilla Regiment and has tackled many enemies. The Japanese forces are moving ahead from the Irrawaddy river. Netaji, too, is moving ahead with his force. For them, it is a joyous occasion; they are doing something for their country—be it to kill or be killed. Despite this, the status of the war is depressing. Netaji will not accept defeat, regardless of the destination of the Japanese forces. He states that even though the friendship between Japan and the Azad Hind Government will last forever, our freedom is *ours* alone. The blood of Indians will colour the path to Delhi and we will garland the Red Fort with the tricolour.

February 1945[18]

Winter, but this is Tokyo. Spring is a while away. A white blanket of snow covers the earth and it feels as though the sky will burst into tears at any moment. Here and there, evergreen trees show the tips of their fingers. It is cold. We know dawn will rise tomorrow, but today, if conditions stay the same, we will freeze to our bones. There is no strength left in the gas stove. We make tea for Ma with whatever wood remains, without milk. Hunger gnaws at us, but there is nothing to eat. Ma bartered a cotton sheet for rice some days ago in the village of Kokubunji, but there is only a handful left of it now. When Ashok doesn't care about his hunger, how can I say I am starving? When Baby sings, how can I cry about hunger? When nothing worries Ma, then how can I, her eldest daughter, no, her *eldest*, make a face? Ashok is only eight.

On our way to college, there is an attack, and we rush into a trench. Looking up, we see a throng of American B-29 bombers hovering over us. We call them Mosquitoes—because they make a buzzing sound on approach and are smacked down to the ground like pests. Here they come, swarm after swarm, their propellers slicing the thin air. Two Mosquitoes and one Japanese airplane are on fire. They glide smoothly towards the ground, one after the other. The Japanese pilot, sun glinting against his green wings, waves his handkerchief, bidding farewell to the world. Taking leave from the red sky and the white earth, he becomes a martyr. In his mind, he has probably made a vow to be reborn in his holy motherland, Nippon. How brave he is! I wish I could attain a similar death.

After college, I visit the ration office; I have a permit which allots us five hundred grams of Burma rice. Ishikawa-san says they have received five kilograms of rice for ten households, meaning five hundred grams per house. At least we get to see rice after a month. I also get a pack of cigarettes. I gather the rations and head home, thinking I'll give the cigarettes to the grandfather in our tonarigumi; he lives alone since his three sons are in the battlefield. He lost his wife earlier.

As soon as I return home, the siren begins to howl—*bo-bo-bo-bo*. The enemy pilots have reached the periphery of Tokyo. In a few minutes, carpet-bombing will begin. Snatching the bag of priceless rice along with a first-aid kit and a helmet filled with cotton, I rush to the trenches with Tulu. The Mosquitoes arrive soon after, dual sirens screeching around us. Bombing begins almost immediately. The air heaves and the earth shudders. From the ground, the Japanese try their best to retaliate with their anti-aircraft guns. Japanese fighter planes roar upwards and the calm evening sky bleeds rust. Intense fighting breaks out. Tulu and I quietly exit the trench. It is difficult not to be curious, despite Ma's instructions. She has forbidden us from coming out of the trenches.

The spectacle is truly entertaining: imagine thousands of needles piercing the sky, a tapestry, a theatre like no other. Cinder and fire. Flaring planes, both American and Japanese, engaged in a duel to death.[19] Watching the scene unfold, we, too, wish to hoist ourselves onto the burning cinders and cry with joy. They say war is a catastrophe. But those brave hearts who fight for their nation—be it to win or to die—are divine.

The skies eventually become calm and, as the earth smoulders, we return to our home. The government has forbidden us from lighting a candle or producing any sort of light. Only a traitor would light a flame—or a cigarette—at this moment. Holding Ma's shoulders, we bring her to the room and gather around her. Soon, the radio informs us that the enemy has left Japanese territory.

Ma's shadowy figure places something in our hands.

I cry out: 'Ma, where did you find this bread?'

'First, you all eat.'

'Ma, where is yours?' Ashok asks.

He worries about Ma first, his hunger last. We break our bread into smaller pieces and feed her. After finishing our princely meal in darkness, we wash ourselves and slip under our blankets. Tonight, unlike other nights, Ma is not talkative. Nor does she gently scold us. Who knows what suddenly happens to her? So joyful and busy, and then unexpectedly, a stony silence that petrifies us. She sings—sometimes in Bengali, sometimes songs of prayer, sometimes Rabindra Sangeet, and abruptly, during a verse, her voice breaks and she collapses into tears. We are too scared to ask her the reason.

Tuesday, 13 February 1945

We receive news from the Japanese headquarters. Papa and some of his companions are coming—today itself. It is absolutely white outside, as though all houses and trees in our neighbourhood have covered themselves with cotton from head to toe.

We go to the station without Ma.

She says: 'I'll keep the food ready; return quickly.'

Papa arrives at the station in his INA uniform. Usually, whenever he returns from his tours, Tulu jumps and dangles from him, but this time, neither does Tulu jump nor does she embrace him. Papa himself puts a hand on her shoulder and they walk together to the car. Papa and I understand Tulu's mental state. For several weeks, she has been looking disheartened. She sings, laughs and does her work, but her eyes are hollow and filled with sadness. This is all my fault. I am leaving.

We go to Tokyo Hotel and meet all of Papa's companions. We are walking up to Papa's room when suddenly the siren bleats—

bo-bo-bo-bo—and then immediately the sound changes, indicating that enemy planes are overhead. Bombing begins and we rush underground. We have our lunch in the basement of the hotel—balls of rice stuffed with pickled Japanese plum. For us, simple as it may be, the meal is a feast.

Papa is busy talking to other Indians. He shares inspiring and heart-wrenching news of the previous year, the amazing feats of the INA and Netaji on the Burma front in 1944—stories woven together with threads of hope and despair.

But we repeatedly remember Ma waiting for us alone at home. How can we remind Papa? He is not ours alone, but belongs to everyone. At three in the afternoon, the hotel staff serve us tea and sandwiches. Out of courtesy, we remain seated in silence, and when Papa tells us to eat, we delicately hold a sandwich between two trembling fingers and press it between our lips. If we were at home, we would have emptied the plates by now.

The bombing stops. To pass time, we take a round of the hotel and return. When it's time to leave, we head to the hotel exit and see Papa chatting with Rama Murti Kaka.

He turns to us and says: 'I'm coming; you both wait here.'

My foot! I immediately understand we are not going to return home today. Papa has pressing work; even then, the least he can do is let us go home. The female staff of the hotel have given us kimonos to wear and a spring mattress for us to sit on while we wait for him.

Papa returns only at eight in the evening. He sees us and laughs like a convict. 'As soon as the day breaks tomorrow, we will go to Mama-san.'

I agree, but Tulu protests with a scowling face: 'There are no bombs falling; we can go right now.'

We say 'Jai Hind' to Papa and fall asleep. At home, we cannot sleep without spreading proper sheets on our tatami mats. Here, on the spring mattress, it feels as though we are sinking into ourselves.

Wednesday, 14 February 1945

As soon as we wake up in the morning, we get ready and head towards the railway station. And once we reach the station, the howl of sirens interrupts us again. Papa quickly ushers us into a trench. He spends his time amusing us and the other Japanese people in the trench with stories from the front. He tells us about how he got dysentery in the jungles of Burma and had to be hospitalized.

Netaji came to see how he was doing and said: 'Why, Sahay?'

Papa responded: 'I ate too many mangoes.'

Netaji roared: 'Do you think you will not get time to eat mangoes after independence? We need to go to Imphal. Get well soon and stop eating mangoes till we gain freedom.'

The bombs have stopped. And see this, the trains have also stopped. A train coming from Shinjuku was the target of American bombs, and many were injured and killed. Without trains plying, we can either walk home from here, or head to Shinjuku, then take a bus to Ogikubo and then walk home.

From Ma's diary…

'They still haven't arrived. His friends must have surrounded him. Poor Tulu and Asha must be waiting. I've dug the earth and taken out the moong dal and jeera. It has not spoilt yet.'

Ma has placed Papa's home slippers under a chair with his yukata (an informal evening robe) folded neatly nearby. From the kitchen, the scent of Indian food—must be the smell of cumin seeds frying.

Papa enters the kitchen and smiles like a mischievous boy. 'We got a little late.'

We all shake with laughter. Moong dal, aloo bhaji, and after many days, Ma in a saree.

A joyous atmosphere, and even in the cold of February, the smell of spring.

Thursday, 15 February 1945

Papa is with us. He will go to Tokyo city today and will return late. My freshly sewn RJR uniform has arrived. Baby and Ashok have been called back from their school in Niigata-ken. All of us take a photograph together.

A few days later[20]

There is a farewell ceremony for me at 4 p.m. in my college. I have to sit with the principal on the stage today, not with my friends. I don't like this special treatment.

I say to Hitomi-sensei: 'I am going to fight for my country—what need is there for a ceremony?'

Mid-sentence, the sensei cuts me short and pats my shoulder: 'Fine, fine, just come with me…'

I suppose, in any case, I will have to bid farewell to my friends, companions and teachers today.

Hitomi-sensei gives a speech praising Indian culture and the miracle of Azad Hind governance. He speaks of Papa's selfless efforts in creating a bridge of friendship and understanding between Japan and India, and then, at the end, praises me as well. I turn red with embarrassment. Am I worthy of praise? After all, the girls facing me are dealing with adversities of their own. It is my good fortune that I have received the opportunity to join the Indian National Army.

He asks me to rise and say a few words. I feel weak, as though I may collapse at any moment. What will the senior girls say, looking at me?

I whisper: 'I won't be able to speak.'

But the sensei doesn't agree. And I have to stand. I say: 'Thinking about the fact that I have to leave you and go far saddens me. But for you and me alike, serving our nation is our religion; we must fulfil our duty towards our country. When you pray, please pray for India's independence too. This is my only request. Sayonara.'

In the large hall, amid a sea of bent heads, white blouses and blue slacks, a ripple of white handkerchiefs flutter. I can hear soft sniffling. I sit absolutely still, as though made of stone. At the instructions of the sensei, we stand for the Japanese national anthem '*Kimigayo*', and after that I sing the national anthem of the Azad Hind Government, '*Shubh sukh chain ki barkha barse*'.

We disperse, and I walk ahead of my group. The senior girls, who usually distance themselves from us junior girls, come to say sayonara.

They say: 'Asha-san, don't lose. When you reach Delhi, call us, too.'

They gift me a haramaki as a memento, a piece of cloth that is tied around the waist. Japanese women usually give this talisman to soldiers before they leave for the battlefield. The cloth is one-metre long and laced with a hundred red stitches sewn by one hundred different women.

From college, we go to the hostel and our photographs are taken. First, with my best friend, Suzuki-san, and then with the rest of my group.[21] This is followed by a photograph with our seniors, teachers and the hostel superintendent.

I return home at seven in the evening. Ma and Tulu are busy with housework. Ma doesn't give me any work to do any more.

'Arre baba, if you cut your hand here, how will you work there?' she says.

Papa overhears us and says: 'What, is she going to her in-laws that you're not letting your daughter work?'

Ma retorts quickly: 'You be quiet!' She then smiles and speaks before going to the living room. 'Netaji's soldier will hold a gun in her hand, not a flower.'

End-February 1945[22]

Bombs are falling over Tokyo continuously now. Ma still does not let me do any work around the house. Whenever I try to do anything, she instructs me to stop. She speaks to me lovingly, but after living in such a disciplined manner for so many years, this care and concern seems strange.

Ma says to me: 'Look, Asha, I have already handed over your father and uncle to Mother India. Now you, too, are no longer my daughter, but India's daughter. You must forget all of us and follow Netaji's orders. Yes, and remember, being my Asha, never do anything that will make people laugh at your Papa and Ma.'

She continues: 'In India, when a daughter's marriage is arranged, her mother keeps her away from all activities involving fire, where she could get hurt. I'm not worried about whether you will go to your in-laws or not; however, your body now belongs to Mother India and hence, I will protect you from now itself.

'One more thing, you are leaving your home. You are intelligent. However, you are still a teenager, a bookworm. How will you tell men apart? It is very difficult to recognize men. Just remember one thing—never be alone, always be with two–three people, and, if you face any adversity, then remember me. I will pray for your well-being.'

I don't know why she's so worried. I am going to fight. I will have a gun in my hand. Aside from the British, everyone else will be my friends. Anyway, I will remember Ma's words.

End-February to March 1945[23]

My eyes open at 5 a.m. Tulu is working mechanically. I go to lend a hand.

'Just go from here...' she says, turning her face away.

Ma is chirping like a little girl, singing Rabindranath Tagore's song '*Baje vidai shuru*'. Let the songs of farewell commence. I am cruel; I am leaving these people today. Baby and Ashok are singing because their eldest sister is going to fight for freedom. But I cannot bear to see Tulu in this state. Our relationship, the relationship of two sisters, has always been such that this farewell is bound to be especially painful. Nonetheless, I have to forget myself. The sadness of others cannot concern me. My sole aim is to serve the nation.

By the time I had finished kindergarten and had started going to school, Tulu had already turned five. Every day, from morning to evening, she incessantly repeated, 'When will Asha return?' Ma eventually got irritated. Fed up, one day, she brought Tulu to school. After speaking to the headmaster, she got permission for Tulu to sit next to me. Ever since then, I have looked after her: from getting her ready in the morning to arranging her school bag, it's been my work alone. If either of us were to get sick, I know Tulu would give up her life for me as I would for her. If either of us ever made a mistake, and Ma–Papa asked us what happened, Tulu always took the blame and tried to save me from punishment.

Sometimes, I was mischievous. I took advantage of Tulu's love and remained silent. Ma, of course, knew and tried to get rid of this mischievousness by explaining things matter-of-factly and giving me a gentle spanking. But I never gave Tulu a punishment on purpose. That's why I was astonished whenever I got scolded.

When I became older, I came to my senses. In school, they organized sports activities by age. However, Tulu and I always wanted to race together. The whistle blew and ten girls began running. Normally, Tulu was quick, but today she hurt her leg and the space between us widened. When I saw I had left her far behind, I ran back, held her hand, and we raced together. This was against the rules, and we came last. Soon, it was time for prize distribution. The chief guest first called us both forward. We fearfully approached his table. Ma was there, too, getting worried. We received the first prize.

The headmaster said: 'Today, we have gained an ideal. This is an example of teamwork. And that's why we've given these sisters the first prize.'

The spectators, both children and parents, seated under tents in the school compound, applauded loudly. We remained standing, shrivelling with embarrassment. Now, we have both become older and can understand the world. Even then, Ma and Papa still think of us as children and explain sundry matters.

***

We have had breakfast. I have set my frock aside, and have worn my INA uniform, including my cap and boots.

I go along with Ma to say goodbye to the neighbours. Then we leave our lane in Ogikubo and walk towards the station. Behind us, our neighbours follow holding the Japanese Hinomaru flag and the Indian tricolour, chanting, 'Banzai, banzai'. At the station, two of my good friends come to see me off. We stand around, waiting for the 8 a.m. train. We try to remain upbeat, but with time, shades of sorrow cloud our faces. Ma remains quiet, occasionally looking at me admiringly. I don't have the courage to look at her, knowing I will collapse into tears. I remember a couplet: 'You, who live on the moon, don't shed tears here'. A Sindhi friend of Papa's had recited it to us once. Soldiers do not have permission to cry.

My eyes meet Ma's, and she smiles bravely. I turn away. Both my friends stand near Tulu, chatting with her. Tulu replies in monosyllables. Tsutomu's elder sister, Aiko-san, sometimes smiles and speaks and sometimes becomes sad, like the moon playing hide and seek with the clouds.

Tsutomu stands beside me and gently says: 'Asha-san, I am coming, too. Till then, keep destroying the enemy.'

I am quiet. He gives me a red rose. I will keep it in my diary forever.

It looks like my best friend Suzuki-san will break down at any moment. All I can say to her is that we will meet again in Free India. And when we meet, we will sing.

Again, we fall silent. Why is parting so painful? It's difficult to add any happiness to the moment. When someone arrives, there is happiness. But when they depart, they leave pain and sadness in their wake. Parting must be painful for birds and animals, too. A lioness must lose her mind upon losing a lion. A cow must become teary-eyed upon losing her calf. Upon gaining a master, a dog wags his tail, and upon losing him, he creates a mournful atmosphere everywhere. Then, how can an intelligent, societal animal like man deprive himself of the same emotions? We try our best to make this emotion secondary—unsuccessfully.

I have stayed away from Ma several times. The first time was in 1939, when Ma went to India and left us with a servant named Shige-san. We called her Onee-san, meaning elder sister. I was twelve years old and Tulu was ten. Baby and Ashok were younger, and Ma took them with her.

Ma had to take a very important message to Netaji. Papa had verbally told Ma the message, making it a point of not writing it down, and sent her to India. The ship left Kobe harbour and went westwards, breaking apart the red and green tape. When the farewell horn started blowing, Tulu started screaming and crying: 'I want to go to Mama-san!'

I don't know whether to call it restraint or cruelty or heartlessness, but not a single tear fell from my eyes. Instead, Tulu's cries irritated me. We stayed away from Ma for a year. In all this time, I felt her absence only once.

We had a tutor. Sometimes, she was very harsh with me. There was a handpump in our house, and there was a rule that everyone had to pump it fifty times. But she made me pump it a hundred times. In these moments, I would remember Ma.

However, Ma's experience in India was very thrilling—about which we learnt much later.[24] Her mission was top secret, and it began with Ma and Papa pretending to be separated. All of Kobe believed they had failed to live with each other. Ma was to return to India with Baby and Ashok, as a bitter, separated wife. As soon as she reached Calcutta, she accommodated herself in a small flat in Shyam Bazaar. She purposely did not stay at her mother's house as it was continuously watched by the CID (Criminal Investigation Department) and moving about would be difficult. Sometime later, she contacted Netaji Subhas Chandra Bose's mother, Prabha Devi, by phone and requested to meet Netaji, who was bedridden and under house arrest since his return from Mandalay. Prabha Devi agreed and, the next day, she sent a car (the famous grey Audi Wanderer) to bring Ma over.

It was a little before midnight, and Ma, seated in the car, noticed a yellow taxi following her. She knew it was the CID. Prabha Devi was waiting for Ma at the portico of the family home on Elgin Road. She embraced Ma and took her into Netaji's room.

After touching his feet, Ma started narrating their activities in Japan. She informed him that Papa was eager for Netaji to join them in East Asia and lead the movement. He had specifically sent her to Calcutta to request him to join them.

Papa had planned for Netaji to escape from India and reach Japan via Germany. He had already consulted the German ambassador in Japan for assistance.

Netaji agreed instantly. He informed Ma that he would start making plans as soon as he recovered. Ma was overjoyed. She paid her respects to both Netaji and Prabha Devi, and breathed a sigh of relief now that her mission was complete.

She returned to the flat in Shyam Bazaar, and entered the room where Baby and Ashok were fast asleep. She bent down and patted the cheek of Ashok when a loud noise rattled the front door. She crept out of the children's room and opened the door cautiously.

A Bengali moshai was standing at the threshold.

'Didi, I want to ask you some questions,' he began.

Ma interrupted him angrily: 'Is this the time to visit a lady? Are you a gentleman? How dare you? If you want to talk to me, come tomorrow morning at nine. Now go!'

She knew very well that he was with the CID.

The next morning, exactly at 9 a.m., the moshai arrived. He started asking her questions: 'Excuse me, but who is Anand Mohan Sahay? Who is he to you?'

Ma raised an eyebrow. 'You know everything and yet you're asking me?'

'Well, why are you here? Why did you visit Subhas Babu?'

'You know he is very ill and bedridden. I am his cousin sister. Is it wrong to visit an ailing brother? Please do not ask foolish questions. Now, you can have a cup of tea and go.'

The man looked embarrassed. 'Sorry, Didi; this is my job. I must know everything and report—'

'Report to your boss, no? Very good! Please make your boss happy.'

'I have a family to maintain. I get a salary for this…'

'And I also have children, but I am no stooge of the British! Well, have your tea and leave.'

As her mission was now complete, Ma planned for her return to Kobe. She went to Writers' Building for her passport the next day. At the gate of Writers' Building, the guards stopped Ma by crossing their bayonets. Ma simply passed under the two rifles and reached the office. The guards gaped, their mouths open in astonishment.

At the office, the passport clerk could not find her passport and was delaying the process. He was about to excuse himself, citing his inability to find the passport, when she pulled it up from under some other papers. The clerk again started giving excuses. Ma picked up the receiver and called her cousin, Mukherjee Babu, (a senior officer at the Passport Office), and brought his attention to the dilly-dallying tactics of the clerk. He at once ordered the clerk to take the necessary steps and asked Ma to come up to his office on the third floor. She went up and, while chit-chatting, received the passport brought up by the clerk. She thanked him and came out of the building.

The same Bengali moshai with the CID was waiting outside the gate. The guards did not misbehave this time.

'Well, what's the matter?' Ma asked him. 'Are you not fed up of following me? Oh, you are on duty! Poor thing! Well, I am going back to Kobe. We will meet again in Free India, then?'

The man looked sheepish. 'Namaskar, hope to meet you again.'

Ma had to wait a few days before boarding the ship. As she was not to meet her mother, Urmila Devi, or any other relatives, she spent the days enjoying herself by going to the theatre and taking the children to the zoo. She was very comfortable, even though she had to face the harassment of the CID several times.

At last, the day to be reunited with her elder daughters and her husband arrived. She boarded the ship with her children and, as soon as they entered the cabin, four CID officials pushed their way in. They wanted to search her. Apart from searching through her baggage, they wanted to search through her hair, which was rolled into a bun! Ma calmly told them to wait. She went out to call Dr Gupta, the ship's doctor, also a family friend.[25] Dr Gupta came to the cabin and chided the CID officials. He asked them to get off the ship as soon as possible. The ship started sailing and Ma, Baby and Ashok finally relaxed.

The ship arrived at Shanghai seaport. Papa came aboard to meet Ma, Baby and Ashok, but sadly he had to stay back in Shanghai. He was organizing a new branch of the Indian Independence League there.

The second time I was away from Ma was when I went to study in Tokyo. I went for a duration of six months with Shige-san. I was fourteen years old, and I distanced myself from everyone. I would be happy sitting alone and dreaming. Shige-san took care of my meals and helped me get ready for college. She was less a servant and more an elder sister to me. Perhaps because of her affection, I didn't realize Ma's absence too much. One day, when I returned home from college, I saw several types of dishes displayed on the table—a cake, pastries, Japanese sweets and a lot more. That morning, I had remembered that it was my birthday but ... because I was away from Ma, I didn't feel like celebrating. Shige-san asked me to change my clothes. She called my friends over. We spent the evening laughing and singing.

***

The train arrives. Papa and I stand at attention and salute everyone. Slowly groaning to life, the train begins moving. Someone says 'banzai', the Japanese equivalent of 'may you have a long life', and someone else shouts 'Jai Hind'. Soon all faces become hazy and then distant.

I am preparing myself for a new chapter, new people, a new environment. I must look absent-minded, but no one is hounding me with concern. My mind is hollow. I stare out of the window at the bright green fields, still covered with snow here and there. Now, I think, I can sing any patriotic song—Japanese, Hindustani, or Bengali—openly. I start mumbling '*Sarthak janam amar*'—my ideal life.

Papa is sitting on another berth chatting with Rama Murti Kaka. He first asks me if I am remembering Ma and then reminds me that I've become a soldier. I become angry. I am not in the habit of chiding my elders so I remain quiet. But I cannot help but think that he himself must be thinking about Ma; how can he give me advice?

Papa again begins chatting with Rama Murti Kaka in Hindi. I look out of the window. Some children are waving their hands amid a destroyed city. These children, born in times of war, are playing a game—seeing how close they can come to the train. Who knows when they'll stop trains again? Who knows when the demon's bullets will rain on these children? It's as though this burnt city is showing me stories of my own grief and suffering.

After passing through Nagoya and Kyoto, we reach Kobe at eleven in the morning.[26] A group of Indians arrive at the station to greet us. We take a vehicle to Oriental Hotel. At 1 p.m., after lunch, we lie down on the princely beds of the hotel. I make note of the Japanese poem I had composed on the train.

The shadow of smoke
wanders through the fields, shining
under the rays of a new spring.

Fuji, snow-capped,
and today, the last welcome
of the stars for me.

What can you or I do?
Memories never leave,
teardrops, Ma's bindi—edged away
only to return.

I am familiar,
I have adopted it all:
a soldier's walk, clothes,
but a strange sadness
still lingers somewhere,
in my mind, my heart, my pen.

Turn back and see, the
country of Fujiyama,
a patriotic path,
admired protectors,
sacrificing oneself, and on
to the battlefield.

Brother, come tomorrow,
young hands, wave a flag first, then
think of lifting guns.

Part Two

Thursday, 22 March 1945

After many years, I am returning to the place of my birth, to the small wooden home in Kinochi where Ma and Papa first brought me home from the hospital. Who knows if it's still there or if it too has turned to ashes? I have a strong urge to visit my teachers and companions from school in Uozaki. I tell Papa: 'Let's go tomorrow. We can meet everyone.' Papa mumbles okay and falls asleep. It's astonishing—life is full of dangers; one can't talk about tomorrow when we don't know what will happen today. Yet, he always remains unperturbed, forever happy like a child. Even when he sleeps, he is absolutely calm and at peace. I write a letter to Ma.

My Mother,

Now I have truly gone. Yesterday, we reached Oriental Hotel at eleven. There was nothing to do. I spent the day arranging my gifts and mementos. I keep remembering Tokyo. You had said that I will remember you at some point. Ma, ever since all your faces faded from my sight at the railway station, I have kept myself determined. Even then, your face keeps appearing before me. I know you will scold me profusely in your next letter and all my weaknesses will disappear. Whenever I face any difficulties or am sad, I will forever remember you and steel myself.

The situation in Kobe—after the bombing of 19 February, houses are still burning here and there. The sky is red in the east. Something else must be burning further ahead. Naraindas' office, the Indian Independence League, everything is destroyed. Our Japanese dolls must have been burnt, too. There is no water in the taps, but it looks like the sky will cry at any moment. I can neither see the hills of Rokko-san nor Awaji Island. Like this sky, I, too, am becoming emotional.

I have tea with milk and sugar three or four times a day. If possible, I will send some sugar to you via Rama Murti Kaka. Please do not worry about me or else you will fall sick. If you worry, then I will also worry and will be unable to learn how to fight. Your strength is my strength. Our health and bodies are for our country alone. That's why we must make the promise to not waste time worrying, alright?

Jai Hind!
Yours only,
Asha

My dear Tulu,

We may have parted, but will continue to meet in our letters. You have now become the eldest sister. Please take care of Ma from my side too. Don't let yourself get sad. Yesterday, I had Indian food—pooris. But when I remember you all, I lose my hunger immediately. The bombs have shattered Kobe even more than Tokyo. Mud has subsumed everything. There is electricity now, but no water. I have not yet made a mistake. When I do, I will let you know. Always be Ma's dutiful daughter, and Baby and Ashok's good sister.

Jai Hind!
Your Asha

Dear Ashok,

I have kept your tricolour flag safely in my suitcase. I will fight on your behalf. Till then, you keep studying. Don't cry at small things. Listen to everyone. In this hotel, there are lots of children like you. Their homes have been burnt down, and they've lost their mothers and fathers. The American devils have stolen everything from them. Even then, no child is crying. They all say they will grow up and kill the enemy. You, too, grow up quickly and come south.

Yours,
Asha Didi

Dear Sumona,
Now, I am truly going. South. Who knows when we will meet again? Yes, when you turn sixteen, you should also come. You'll have to become very strong from now itself. Don't study too much and ruin your health. I saw your report; you've got lots of marks. Great job! My pen is with Tulu. Keep it as something to remember me by.

Yours,
Asha Didi

Friday, 23 March 1945

I rise at seven this morning. We go to Mangalmalji's house. We speak about staying here. He has a Japanese wife and children. From a Japanese perspective, the house is well-furnished. I can smell Indian food upon entering. On the table, I see dry lentils and a yellow flower. A song by Devika Rani plays on the gramophone. Obasan (Aunty) is making doughnuts. She teaches me, as well. After making a few, I start laughing. What is the point of learning how to make doughnuts? I need to learn how to fire bullets. She then begins gifting me small Japanese trinkets.

I say, Obasan, what will I do with all of this?

She tells me to take it, and, if I feel like giving it away, I should. She then tells me not to worry.

Me and worry? That's a habit that belongs to cowards! I am one of those who will laugh till my dying breath.

We go to Uozaki. The village of Sumiyoshi. The stream that flowed from the front of our house into the ocean continues to flow in the same manner. But our house has been burnt to the ground. We go to my old school and discover that all the teachers are new. When we ask about the old teachers, we are told they have all gone south for the war. I walk on the ground where we used to play basketball. The same soft sand. A map of Japan made of cement. It is the same—rainwater still pools in its centre. Outside the school, I can see the stationery shop where we bought buns for our tiffin. The same old man is there. I am in my INA uniform and people look at me curiously.

We go to the local Shinto temple of our neighbourhood and press our hands together. I used to visit this temple and pray for the victory of our country and the well-being of our soldiers. The cleanliness of the temple was the responsibility of the students of my school. We were divided into groups, and each group was assigned one week's duty to clean the temple and its yard.

We then go to meet our old neighbours. First, we go to Ishi Obasan's house. She is a good friend of Ma's. She enquires about Ma, and then serves us tea and sweets. I tell her I am going off to war. She chats with us—sometimes crying, sometimes laughing. We bid her goodbye, meet a few other neighbours and then leave. Feels as though life has become an endless series of goodbyes. We return to Kobe from Uozaki.

My guess turns out to be correct—our hotel room is filled with guests. The air is hazy with the smoke of cigarettes and politics. I open a window to let pure air enter. Everyone is so engrossed in political debates that they don't even realize the windows are shut.

A little while later, we go to a Buddhist temple named Gokuraku-ji. We pay obeisance to a human-sized statue of the Buddha and then return to the hotel. Gokuraku means heaven.

At 5 p.m., there is a meeting at the India Club. All the Indian residents of Kobe, aside from Mr Sadani, are present. We have heard that he has done something against the Japanese government and has been imprisoned. Poor Jameesha and her cow-like mother. I am truly fortunate to be born to parents like Ma–Papa. They stitched patriotism into us before we were born. Their goal from the very start has been to attain freedom for India, and until then, they swear to be restless. Looking at the wives of merchants, drowning in revelry, instantly angers me. India's freedom does not concern them. Instead, they enjoy pomp and pageantry—georgette sarees, high heels, champagne pearls and sparkling jewels. They seem quite brainless.

Nonetheless, some of them are quite daring. Mrs Kotak and Mrs Futehally have been working with Ma for a long time. Ma once told me the story of how the Indians of Kobe decided to hoist the tricolour from their homes on 26 January 1935. This was a difficult and daring act in those days. That morning, Ma speedily exited our home, a matchbox in hand, and checked if every Indian had hoisted the tricolour or not.[27] She found that all homes except three—that of a Sindhi, a Bengali, and a Punjabi—were flying the tricolour. Ma went to their gates, lit a match, and burnt down the Union Jack.

The three Indians were horrified. They immediately complained to the British Consulate, who reported Mrs Sati Sahay's 'unimaginable crime of insulting the British Crown' to the Japanese authorities.

The Japanese officials nonchalantly told the British Consulate: 'We, Japanese, do not punish or arrest patriots. Mrs Sati Sahay is a great patriot and is fighting for the liberation of her country with her husband and other Indians.' The British Consulate was agitated and asked them to 'arrest the Indian woman and send her back to India'. The Japanese officers declined. Instead of arresting Ma, they praised her profusely. The three Indians were quite ashamed, and, at a meeting held later, they apologized to all the members of the IIL. Ma was honoured and praised for her daring deeds by both the Indian and Japanese residents of Kobe.

Today, when Papa is giving his speech at the meeting, an Indian interrupts him: 'And if the Japanese lose, what will happen to us? What will happen to our assets and wealth?'

Papa laughs and says who knows what will happen tomorrow when we don't know what will happen today. What if a bomb falls on us right now?

A child of six or seven rushes to the front and says: 'Sahay Kaka, I, too, want to go to Netaji. If I die tomorrow, then how will I go?'

Papa lifts him to his chest and asks him to say 'Jai Hind' loudly. The boy scrambles down, stands at attention and proudly says, 'Jai Hind!' The man concerned about his wealth is put in his place.

After Papa's speech, the secretary of the Japanese Foreign Ministry, Mr Watanabe, speaks. He says that Japan and India have been brothers for eras, and will remain so in the future. Because of our mutual understanding and hard labour, not only Japan and India, but all of Asia will attain freedom.

End-March 1945

We leave for the station at 8.30 p.m. We say goodbye to Kobe and head towards Nagasaki. Then on to Formosa (Taiwan).

Kobe, the place of my birth, once so peaceful. Now the fields here, too, have become fuel for fire. Mt Rokko, where we used to go for picnics, stands the same, quiet as always.

The destruction of Kobe

By demonic feet,
a city crushed, we left you
forever. You will
bloom again, certain
are the saplings of new dreams.
Sprout, if there are seeds,
then this destruction,
this ash, will rise. And again
we will awaken.

The next day

This morning, we arrived in Taihoku (Taipei). We are staying in a modern hotel—a Western-style room with a flush toilet. There is nothing in the Japanese or Chinese style here. Yes, the people speak Japanese, and I chat with the hotel girls. Taihoku is a well-organized and modern city, but fear and apprehension shadows the faces I see. Will the catastrophe of war swallow this quiet island, too?

Mid-April 1945

We have spent twenty-five days in the hotel. Papa is teaching me both Hindi and English. To be honest, anything, including a bomb falling on my head, will be easier than learning how to write Hindi. Even a BA exam in Japanese is easier than writing in Hindi. And I still have to fight for India, so I'm even forbidden from dying at this moment!

Now and then, bombs fall and we have to go to the trenches; the trenches here are at the centre of the roads. We can't sacrifice our valuable bodies to the enemy's bombs just yet. Kill and kill and kill.

Sometimes, I visit the Japanese military camp with Papa. All the officers and soldiers look so rigid and solemn that I find it difficult to even squeak. If anyone asks me anything, I first gulp and then reply. You can't hear a sound other than the click of boots, barked orders and affirmative responses. I have met the commander; I notice that when he laughs, only his moustache quivers. Whenever I greet him, I must stifle my giggles. Even then, the corners of my lips dimple in amusement. I only reply in yes or no. Papa also speaks in very polite and measured tones.

We often have to go to the cantonment for news and further arrangements; we are waiting for an airplane to take us to Taichu (Taichung). I observe everything closely, weighing Japanese military authority against Papa's politeness. I notice two types of behaviours—one is that of military officers and politicians who consider their orders final, and the second is that of Papa's—fulfilling one's destiny by remaining balanced and measured. Whenever we visit the cantonment, they hand us a packet of sugar. We send it further to Ma in Japan. We have to reach Netaji, no matter what needs to be done.

A week later

After waiting for several weeks, we have finally found passage to Taichu on a bomber plane. I am the only girl in a sea of men. Looking at the stern faces of these soldiers, I feel an urge to laugh. It feels as though I am the only sane one standing in a circus of madmen. In this throng of soldiers, Papa is the most experienced warrior; yet, despite a hint of sternness, there is always a look of humility on his face. Still, I sense something missing in their expressions. Whatever it may be, I feel like a princess among all these men.

***

We are staying at a Japanese-style hotel (ryokan) called Chiyanno Uchi, which means 'eternal house'. We have a suite with two rooms—one large and one small—on the topmost floor. In the large room, eight tatami mats filled with Japanese straw are spread over the wooden floor and in the smaller room four tatami mats are laid out. There is also a sofa set, towels and a telephone. I lie down on the sofa. Sleep and exhaustion encircle me. Somehow, I have to keep my eyes open for our next meal, which will be served by the amiable staff of the hotel in a while. Despite my tiredness, I force myself to eat because of Papa's presence; I know how much he enjoys watching me stuff myself. This is my only complaint while staying with Papa.

The staff places sweets at our table. I remember Ashok and don't feel the slightest urge to touch them. Ever since Ashok has been conscious of the world around him, he hasn't seen a single sweet, let alone tasted one. In the name of sweets, we used to make patties of rice with saccharine mixed in it, and that too whenever rations were available. This would satisfy the small kids. Baby often used to give her portion to Ashok.

I can see the seedlings of patriotism rising in these children. They know they must endure all kinds of difficulties for the country. Other than the education we've received from our parents, we have also received Japanese education, which focuses immensely on patriotism and nationalism. Today, we are ready to make every sacrifice for our country. Those who do not have national consciousness are the equivalent of hollow puppets, following instructions mindlessly.

I take another round of the hotel. Turns out my room is named 'Matsuno', which means 'pine'. There is a telephone, but it never rings. There is a calling bell, too, but it doesn't work either. I have a bath at 4.30 p.m. The bathroom is designed in Japanese style with black-and-white floor tiles. In the corner is a round bathtub. After bathing, both my body and mind feel refreshed. There are a lot of servants here. Their matron is an elderly woman who everyone refers to as Obasan. Everyone here is very pleasant and brisk. I learn that the owner of the hotel has also achieved martyrdom on the battlefield.

Today, after many days, I sleep on a mattress spread on the floor and not on a bed. The straw mattress looks new. I love the smell of fresh straw. First, I lie down without the mattress. Then Obasan comes and makes me rise. She calls me by the name 'Ojō-sama'.[28]

'You'll catch a cold. Let me lay the mattress.'

I thank her and assist her.

A haiku

Smell of fresh green straw;
a pristine evening of a
new year, a new spring.

Saturday, 21 April 1945

I rise early this morning. I have rarely experienced dawn breaking—birds are chirping in the trees, clouds are swimming across the sky. I can hear the low moo of cows, the boisterous call of roosters passing on the message that morning has arrived in full glory. This is the opposite of Tokyo's dry, dark environment—here, everything is damp and green. I look out of the window. Spending so much time alone, I end up thinking a lot. When I think of home, there is the danger of sinking into a depthless pool of sentimentality. That's why I try to focus on the future.

I am a soldier of Netaji. I must obey his commands. It is forbidden to ask the reason behind any of his orders. But how do I crush these unyielding emotions? I have to scold myself and hold myself accountable. I am no longer a college girl, who can get sad or upset at insignificant matters.

I start singing nationalistic songs, first in Japanese and then in Bengali ... '*Urdha gagane baaje madol...*'

Who knows for how long Papa has been standing quietly behind me?

Laughing, he asks: 'Did you go to Tokyo to meet Mama-san?'

I become angry. Why can't I keep myself restrained? Why do I keep losing my temper? I stand up straight, and say: 'No, Papa. I was looking outside.'

* * *

Taichu is Formosa's old capital. It used to be a stunning city. Even today, on the outskirts of the city, you can see the remnants of the old kingdom. The sides of the roads are now full of trenches. Between the houses and shops, there are still a few fields remaining. The shops remain shuttered. Signboards have become nesting grounds for birds. The few shops that remain open sell only bamboo commodities. The country produces a lot of bamboo. In the rural areas, villagers spend their time creating bamboo products whenever they get time in between sowing and reaping. In Japan, it's hard to find even a single bamboo bag or basket, and here there are so many.

A stationery shop is open. I know its shelves will be empty, but I cannot resist entering.

An old gentleman sits behind a table at the shop. 'I have some notebooks,' he says, bending to his knees. 'Would you like one?'

I am ecstatic to see a new notebook. In Tokyo, we sometimes received notebooks (of inferior paper) in our ration; we would write with a pencil in them. Here, seeing a fresh notebook, I start jumping with joy—even though it, too, doesn't have great quality paper.

The gentleman continues, 'The notebook is good for writing, but smokers have a tough time with their cigarettes—the moment you light it, it extinguishes. Well, better than nothing, I guess.'

Since our arrival, there has been incessant bombing. The people of Taichu had faith that the enemy would never attack them, but now that belief has faded. Most people have left the cities for the safety of villages in far-off locations.

A few hours later, I return to our hotel and have a novel experience. We are sitting in the living room when suddenly a machine-gun bullet bursts through the window and smashes into the broken telephone. Fortunately, Papa and I had moved a little to the side or else the bullet would have undoubtedly blown our heads off.

* * *

There are a lot of Japanese soldiers staying at this hotel, but it's so silent that you can't tell. This is because they are part of the elite Kamikaze Special Attack Units. They are here waiting for death.

When the staff gives us the information that one team is going to die tomorrow, I am eager to see them. We go to meet them in an enormous hall. I had heard about, and revered, these heroes in Japan. In the past, I had thought of these men as divine beings. But today, I am standing amidst them. They are all between the ages of eighteen and twenty-five years. The captain looks a little older. They appear childlike with fixed, serene, unsmiling faces. Self-possessed, but not grave. They are unconcerned by our sentimentality and reverence.

On the contrary, we are unprepared. They say to us, we all bloom and wither for the country, so what is there to be emotional about? Our actions are based on our desires. What is extraordinary about this? Today, we are leaving. Tomorrow, someone else will leave. Saying all this, they laugh. It looks like they are off on a holiday somewhere. I feel like a fool for letting myself get swept away in a wave of emotionality. Today is a day coloured in the variegated tones of happiness and strife.

Sunday, 22 April 1945

The absence of hunger. When I longed for rice, it was never visible, and today, I have food in front of me, but no desire to eat. The economic situation in Formosa is good. People here haven't experienced hunger or the lack of food; there is plenty of rice and sugar. In Tokyo, people are not aware that everything is available nearby. My stomach hurts from eating too many sweets. I yearn to rest all afternoon.

Papa sits nearby, engrossed in writing something in Japanese. He repeatedly shows me the difficult Kanji characters, asking me if it looks passable.

It's beautiful, I reply.

To the outside world, Papa is a revered and respected figure. But here—in this hotel room—it feels as though he's a student in the first standard.

In the evening, there is a dance of godlike girls in the temple.

Thursday, 26 April 1945

Today is a day filled with significance. It passes with pleasure. At noon, a team from the Makoto Tokkotai (Truth Special Attack Unit) has its farewell ceremony.[29] We all gather in a hall. Soon, young priestesses, beautifully attired in red hakamas (pleated trousers) and white kimonos, enter. Even today, in Japanese Shinto temples, young maidens, or miko, assist the priests in religious ceremonies. Using a branch of a sakaki tree (*Cleyera japonica*), each boy is sanctified. Then the branch is dipped in a red ceremonial lacquer cup which contains o-toso—a special alcoholic drink—that is dedicated to the heroes. This drink is made only in temples, and people consume it exclusively on auspicious occasions like religious ceremonies or marriages. O-toso is made from an extract of rice.

The heroes look divine—their faces glowing, childlike.

Tomorrow, these flowers will fall from planes into the hellfire of the enemy. Thinking about it fills my heart with pain. They request me to give the special o-toso drink to the heroes. It is my first experience in such a situation, and I hesitate. I feel as though

I am about to do something incorrect. But looking at the youthful faces of the heroes, my doubts immediately disappear. I look at Papa for support. He smiles slightly, giving me consent and courage. In the same way that we place offerings such as flowers and fruit before God, we place the cups of Japanese liquor before the heroes. They thank us and drink the liquid silently.

At first, they all sit peacefully, and then slowly, they start talking and singing songs. We can hear them laughing, but even in the din, their behaviour is appropriate. The youngsters chat reverently with their officers, and sometimes, the senior officers joke with the younger men—but the young men follow etiquette seriously. For those facing death tomorrow morning, everything is forgiven. For the pious, duty is the only religion.

The group captain speaks to me. 'Will you also become a soldier? And destroy the enemy?'

He then fills a cup of o-toso with his own hands and places it before me. I am in a dilemma. It feels unkind to disappoint the heroes who will attain martyrdom tomorrow. And so I touch the cup slightly and place it back down. I look towards Papa and see that same teasing smile.

The heroes then take out their tenugui (small Japanese hand towels), and begin inscribing Japanese characters on them with a brush and black ink.

And then one soldier, Captain Michio Kusaba, takes a yellow thread—the kind used by priests as a symbol of protection—and hands it to me with the tenugui.

'I, in any case, will have to go meet mother tomorrow,' he says. 'Keep this thread with you, and whenever you face any difficulty and cannot find a solution, touch this thread and remember your Japanese brother who sacrificed his life with a smile for his country.'

Someone says: 'Till we gain freedom, do not die, Asha-san.'

My fist tightens into a ball and resolute faith fills my heart.

How incomprehensible is the attitude of these soldiers—for them, death is a game. They are unable to separate life from death; there is no line distinguishing the two. Their attitude belongs to a higher plane. If there is anyone beyond human in this world, they are these men—the greatest of ascetics. Losing one Japanese pilot and one small Japanese aircraft means destroying an important enemy aircraft carrier with thousands of enemy soldiers and hundreds of smaller planes. This is the reason our heroes are throwing their lives away today.

Sometime later, I read what is written on the tenugui:

> 'Asako-dono,
> Good luck for your future and for the freedom of your motherland.
> Asia is one.'[30]
>
> —Captain Michio Kusaba
> 26th April Showa 20th Year,
> Makoto Tokkotai
> Nippon Teikokugun (The Imperial Japanese Army)

The next day, at 4 a.m., Captain Michio Kusaba crashed his plane into the chimney of an American battleship in the seas near Okinawa and attained martyrdom along with the other members of his Tokkotai. With this sacrifice, the enemy troops lost thousands of soldiers. More than five battleships were sunk during this period.

Today, I have had the fortune of witnessing this miraculous scene of Japanese history. Remembering this, I know I will be victorious. The spirit of my brave Japanese brothers will take me to Free India.

Friday, 27 April 1945

We spend the time between 10 a.m. and 3 p.m. outside the city daily. We must stay safe from air attacks. Today, we will visit Lin Shi's palace (Wufeng Lin Family Mansion). Lin Hsien-tang, whose ancestor was Lin Shi, is Formosa's most distinguished and affluent gentleman. Japan's emperor has chosen him to be a member of the Diet, the Japanese parliament.[31]

His house is a surreal, dreamlike palace built in the Japanese Nara style. The residents also wear clothes from this time period. It feels as though we have suddenly entered ancient Japan. There are about twenty portraits of Lin Hsien-tang's ancestors hanging near the entrance. Verandas with red lacquer railings encircle the structure. There are around fifteen beautiful lanterns dangling from the ceiling of the veranda. These are not constructed of glass but of paper and red wooden frames. And standing near the threshold of the door, about three feet apart, are two statues of divine gatekeepers, also made of wood. A unique quality about Asia is that every religious place will have a statue of a gatekeeper. This tradition began in ancient India, and still continues in South India, Tibet, Nepal and other tribal areas. Places of worship in such regions have gatekeepers at their entrances. Thus, this is not an Aryan tradition, but that of the Dravidians and Mongols.

I find the conversation between Papa and Lin Hsien-tang on the shared history of India and Asia very interesting. Papa notices that the architecture of the palace is similar to the type you see in South India. Every aspect of the palace is colourful, and the rays of the southern sun make everything seem brighter and more resplendent. While we are here, I do not even remember the war. I feel like a princess visiting a palace.

'Again, you're lost in your imagination; come back to yourself,' instructs Asha's spirit.

People speak demurely in the house. We meet some of the family elders, including a man with a beard whiter than snow. He is wearing a Nara-era kimono, but it is so long that it falls below his feet and drapes the ground. His obi (sash) is very thin and the kind that is tied at the front.

The old gentleman says, 'I am living the life of an ascetic.'

There are two beautiful girls, too, who speak Japanese. It does not take us time to start chatting. War, hunger, and the aspiration to defeat the enemy—thinking about these things is how I am spending my time in Taichu. But right before jumping into the scorching flames of a fire, I find this sanctuary of peace and prosperity. How strange! I have read stories of princesses, and it feels like I am meeting them in real life. They speak well, their voices tinkling like the sound of a small bell. I'm a quiet person and I do not enjoy noise. But I am not weak. The three of us looked like two princesses and a prince. If I was really a prince, I know these girls would become infatuated with me immediately. I always hold myself straight and, like a prince, have a powerful urge to serve my nation. But again, these pointless dreams. Damn this mind of mine, hovering around such youthful fantasies.

Amid this, Papa asks me for a word equivalent to 'huryu' in English. I immediately joke that there mustn't be such a word in English. It means a man of special emotions in Japanese. Yes, 'style' could be an answer.

Back to modernity from the ancient world. After dinner, we visit Taichu's State Temple. Like Japan, there are many state temples here with priests presiding over them. The priests here are hereditary.

It is a full-moon night and everything is bright. The city, asleep. And we, strolling down the streets, are going towards the temple. Somewhere a cricket, somewhere a night bird, is singing its song. Nearby, a stream is gurgling and giving us company.

Aside from this singing contest, everything is silent. In a bit we can see the torii of the temple. It is very high; at least fifty metres tall, made of rosewood and covered in rust-coloured plaster. A Chinese proverb is inscribed in the middle in gold. This torii is also a gift of Indian architecture and culture.

Papa says, 'Even in India, Buddhist temples have toranas or ornamental gateways at the front. Like the columns and pillars in Sanchi, this column has been made for birds to stay.'

Therefore, in Japanese or Chinese, the word torii means a place for birds to reside. From the torii till the main temple, every surface is studded with bright round stones. Walking up the stairs takes us to a wide veranda, and the roof of the temple is covered with countless golden flowers and leaves. Inside, there are the idols of two gods and one goddess. Papa informs me that the temples in India also have similar statues placed, like that of the Goddess Bhagwati. I pray for the success of our selfless heroes and for the victory of Greater Asia. We return to our hotel, flushed in the light of the moon.

Before entering the sanctuary of my dreams, I have to return to reality. The American demons do not leave us in peace even on this still, moonlit night. They enter with a roaring *bhoo* sound, just like malarial mosquitoes, and then vanish like ghosts.

We have to go to the trenches. The Kamikaze Special Attack Unit heroes also choose to go to the trenches because they don't want to die the needless death of dogs. Among these people, there are also some Japanese soldiers who are taking a stroll. Looking at the moon, they begin composing and singing haikus. A Japanese haiku comprises three phrases of five, seven, and five syllables. Some soldiers begin playing 'robber-robber'. One soldier removes a Japanese sword from his sheath and begins performing a war dance a little distance away. What a sight to behold! Above us, the light of the moon and down below the angry dance of warriors. Japanese soldiers have an artistic attitude. There are some who, before performing hara-kiri or ritual suicide, sit quietly and perform tea ceremonies or ikebana. They view art as a means of attaining peace before entering their next lives.

Sunday, 29 April 1945

Today is the birthday of Emperor Hirohito. This is an important annual festival for the people of Japan, who wish their gentle-hearted king a long life. School and college students assemble and sing the emperor's birthday song.

In the morning, a brave brother from the Tokkotai enters our room and begins asking Papa about India. It doesn't feel as though he is going to die for his country this evening. I keep staring at him

Papa chides me: 'What are you thinking, Asha?'

The brave hero speaks: 'Asha-san, please keep praying that I successfully strike an enemy ship.'

I cannot speak. I place a cup of tea before me and quietly sit down. The moment I try to speak, tears roll down my cheeks.

At 4 p.m., they leave. A little while later, we can see their airplanes above us. They circle over us and flutter their wings, bidding us farewell. Soon, they become distant specks before returning to circle over us again. We wave our handkerchiefs. Eventually my eyes fill with tears and I cannot show my face to Papa; I know he will laugh. But what I see is that he, too, is gently wiping his eyes. This farewell is unforgettable. It is our duty to give peace to the spirits of our brave brothers, who leave us laughing, forever in high spirits. Not just by giving India her freedom, but by freeing all enslaved nations. Only then will their souls find peace. This is not a dream, but a reality.

Monday, 30 April 1945

From tomorrow, May will begin. We are still in Taichu. Who knows when we will reach Burma? Yet, staying here I've had several experiences.

Today, two military officers arrive from the Philippines. They had the honour of reaching the Tokkotai to the enemy ships and witnessing the monumental work they do. In other words, they had the job of reaching them to the jaws of death.

I ask them: 'How do you feel watching the heroes strike the enemy ships?'

'It's impossible to describe this experience in words, Asha-san,' replies one officer. 'What can we say? At that moment, the only words we can utter are, "It is done."'

In reality, asking the question was a sign of my stupidity.

He continues: 'These Japanese pilots have special abilities. They can weave and spin their planes in any direction like leaves. It doesn't even take them a second to drop the plane, and enter the enemy ship's chimneys quickly and efficiently.'

He then gifts me a Japanese fan with the words of the song "Sakura" written on it.

At 3 p.m., we go to a village named Kakoi. Mr Chin, who is travelling with us, takes us to his house. As soon as we reach, Papa begins making his special chicken curry. This is typical of Papa—whenever the opportunity strikes, he cooks chicken; it is something he is very passionate about. An unfortunate chicken meets its end.

I stutter the words, 'Oof, poor thing.'

Papa immediately pounces. 'A soldier should never show sympathy.'

I respond, 'But, Papa, there are so many chicks and their mother has just been killed.'

Papa continues to work quietly. I go for a stroll outside. Till the distant horizon, I can see flowering fields, a few white birds, a scramble of chickens and the dishevelled dogs who are looking after them. A farmer is singing in nasal tones about village life, the beauty of fields and forests. From behind, the children of the village approach and look at me from head to toe with curious eyes. I call them over in Japanese and they flee.

Then I say in Chinese: 'Lai, lai.'

They slowly approach. This is an example of their fear of Chinese authority, which has been here from ancient times, and was a symbol of barbarity. But what has passed is easily forgotten.

When I return, I help Papa prepare the chicken. But my hunger has been satiated by the smell of spices frying. I become stubborn and say I will not eat today. Papa doesn't forcefully attempt to feed me either.

Asia has three great countries: India, China and Japan. There are distinct features in the cuisines of each country. In India, it is flavour. In Japan, the focus is on the presentation of dishes. Papa is chatting with Mr Chin and his family. He says one achieves happiness in life when one's wife is Indian, cuisine is Chinese and home presentation is Japanese.

I say: 'Papa, you have already achieved all this.'

He responds: 'Yes, but Mama-san doesn't make Chinese food at home.'

I laugh and agree. 'Yes, because all you want to eat at home is moong dal and roti.'

Mr Chin asks us about Raja Mahendra Pratap. Papa tells him that the British had murdered Rajaji's family and usurped their land. He somehow escaped to Japan, and now preaches universal brotherhood and world religion. He says if there is mutual love in the world, there will be no more wars, because humanity will be selfless, free of pomp and pageantry. Humanity is the ultimate religion. In my opinion, however, there is no religion greater than the religion of loving your country.

Everyone relishes the curry made by Papa. It starts raining on our way back and the village becomes peaceful. Everyone works leisurely. These farmers who toil away quietly and without complaint are also jewels of the nation.

Mr Chin comes with us to the hotel. The three of us sit together and continue to chat. Mr Chin wants to know more about Netaji.

Papa speaks: 'There is a lot to say, and the moment you see him, you will understand his true mettle. He is endowed with all the qualities of a worthy leader, and is a skilled politician and a firm ruler. For the establishment of the Azad Hind Government, he needed a lot of economic assistance. The Indian diaspora in Asia had contributed to the cause, but there was need for more money, and so we went to Burma to gather donations. Burma's southern delta area is the spinal area for rice production. The rice mills are largely owned by South Indian Chettiars, who are thriving merchants. Some Bengalis are also selling medicines in bulk here.

'We gathered a team of friends and other merchants, including Shri S.M. Bashir and other members of the Indian Independence League. In June 1944, we left on a motorboat and met with the Indian diaspora. Everyone donated liberally and with great excitement to the cause. Gold and jewels were also donated. Several hundred tonnes of rice and rare medicines were donated along with about two crore rupees in cash.

'Despite this, some people said, "Now what will we give? These people are troubling us." Netaji heard this complaint, and organized a meeting of merchants and challenged them with an argument. He said, according to international laws, when a nation is fighting a war then personal property becomes the property of the nation. If you think your house and your wealth are yours alone, then you are delusional and your property is now India's alone. If you do not realize the truth that you are a member of Free India, and both you and I have to do everything for freedom, then another path is ready for you. There are many British in jail. You, too, may give them company. But remember, when we go to live in India, there will be no space for you. You are Indian, doing business and making money here. It is not justifiable for you to run away from your duty. You cannot run away; do not think you can work on your own whims.'

Papa becomes excitable as he narrates some parts of Netaji's argument to Mr Chin.

How bold is our Netaji! Papa continues to describe Netaji's daily routine. 'He can stay up all night working, yes, on the strength of coffee. He can finish three or four cups over the night. He also smokes a lot, an absolute chain-smoker. His doctor complains that he eats a lot of betelnut. He always welcomes tea and plays a lot of badminton. He is also religious to an extent. His bag doesn't contain many things, but does always contain a rosary (tulsi mala) and a copy of the Bhagavad Gita. And a bottle of eau de cologne. In Singapore, he sometimes frequents the Ramakrishna Mission. Over there, he meditates for a couple of hours. Now, how will he find time to sit peacefully in Burma? He becomes so engrossed in his work that he forgets to eat and drink. He loves many animals, but not cats. He has a light-hearted personality and loves to joke around. He has a lot of fun joking with his driver and servants.'

Thursday, 3 May 1945

It is raining today. I have written a poem...

Yogi, protecting your saffron spirit,
we march forward towards victory.

Today, once more,
a team of the Tokkotai
will return to their mothers.

The earth rips open
and subsumes us.
Freedom has awakened
and we will be unconquerable.
What face will I show them?
As I bloom, I am caught
by death and demons.

Today, I remain,
in the country of sunrises;
who knows if I will be here
tomorrow, in the country where
coconuts fall into the waves
of the sea?

I look outside the window and see a mango tree with small fruit hanging. I show Papa, and he says: 'Ah, they will be ripe in two months.' His face blooms with an unknown happiness. Indians are mad about mangoes, something I witnessed in Japan many years ago.

When Ma returned to Japan from India, she brought with her a basket of Malda mangoes from Bhagalpur. The Japanese custom officials were scared that cholera could spread by eating the mangoes or taking them into the city. They gave instructions to throw the basket into the sea. As if Ma and Papa would throw one hundred mangoes into the ocean! It would become an incident truly reminiscent of the historic Boston Tea Party. They called the Indian residents of Kobe to the ship and handed them one mango each. It felt like they were handing out sweets to starving children. I watched with astonishment how they slowly sucked and relished the mangoes. Etiquette and concern went flying in the wind.

We softly said to Papa, in Japanese, that these people were very dirty.

Papa responded: 'There can be no concern about etiquette while eating mangoes.'

* * *

It is now 4 p.m. Another group of heroes from the Makoto Tokkotai depart forever. We race in our cars to the airport and stop near the planes. Looking at us, the pilots approach with smiles, no words left to say. We are silent. They stand at attention, salute and then run to their planes. We wave our hats and, one by one, each plane rises past the clouds and vanishes into the distant sky. I don't know if it is numbness or sadness, whatever it is, but we stand still with smiles on our lips. Drenching heroes in something as light and ordinary as tears is a sin. The air is heavy with auspiciousness. I hope and pray that they succeed in their mission.

We all stand absently, our senses lost, as they take their planes for a spin over us, shaking their wings and then leaving. I remember the story of the resurrection of Christ—when he reappears before his believers. Like these Japanese martyrs, how many of our Indian brothers and sisters have worn the red turbans of martyrdom before returning to the earth? A country which gives its youth the choice of dying for its betterment can never be defeated. The countries of Asia will be independent and victorious; they will need to be victorious, not to be is unforgivable.

With indescribable emotions, we return to the hotel, our minds swarming with thoughts of the martyrs. The people of Formosa place great importance on farewell ceremonies. It feels as though sadness must be present in farewell ceremonies. In Buddhist scriptures, there is a verse which has become a character in the Japanese language—the element is visible. In this moment of separation, the verse returns to me. This world is both infinite and evanescent; it is both eternal and changeable. Connections and separations, joy and nostalgia, rise and fall, life and death—this is the circle of life. Trapped in this circle, man forgets the truth and forgets his duty. He loses peace. There will be peace where there is conscientiousness. Duty is the only religion and loving one's country is the supreme religion. What am I thinking? Our brave brothers must have achieved martyrdom by now.

Friday, 4 May 1945

Today, another group of martyrs were to take their leave. They had left at dawn, but returned in the evening. The enemy had somehow heard of their imminent arrival and had moved elsewhere. One soldier here, thousands of soldiers there. One plane can send a ship full of planes to hell. The enemy's withdrawal is natural.

The men return and quietly retreat to their rooms. They never show their faces. They went to die, and they have returned. Is there anything more shameful for a soldier? I feel regret, but also happiness. We have been given an opportunity to be reunited with the heroes who had been given their last farewell. Papa calls the soldiers into his room. They enter with their heads lowered. Their faces are red with shame.

They ask for our forgiveness: 'We will definitely die tomorrow. Please forgive the mistake we made today.'

'We will die.' Meaning they will achieve their goal by killing themselves. These stirring words make us bow our heads. Who are these people? Gods? The divine spirit himself? If five hundred million Asians had the same hearts, Asia would be victorious.

After dinner, we receive a letter from the Japanese headquarters via a messenger. The letter informs us that we will be heading south by plane tomorrow. Papa is thrilled. His companions are fighting in Singapore and Burma, and he is finding it very difficult to spend his days aimlessly in Formosa. It is against his nature, especially when each day is priceless. In this war for freedom, idleness is a potent enemy. I, too, become happy that I will soon enrol in the Rani of Jhansi Regiment. Yes, I feel unhappy about leaving this beautiful island. But I must say farewell and leave with unforgettable memories.

Mr Chin continues to sit in the living room. Despite our insistence, he does not leave. He will drop us at the airport and then leave.

Saturday, 5 May 1945

I wake up at 3 a.m. We reach the airport and board an enormous bomber. It feels as though, yes, I have entered a war. Suddenly, memories of Ma begin torturing me.

Departure. From simple villagers to forthright soldiers waiting for death, to the hotel staff who looked after them—faces from Taichu flash before my eyes. Apart from the crew, there are ten military officers on the plane, all seated on a bench together. Take off. In a single minute we are again outside Taichu. Three hours later, we reach Canton (Guangzhou). My hands, my feet, my ears—everything is vibrating. We do not have permission to step off the plane even for a second; it's very dangerous here. The Americans attack every hour. They are intent on making this port theirs—whatever it may take. They will find it easier to attack Japan from here. Staying here even a minute longer than necessity dictates means a chance of losing one's life in vain.

We take off again, rising steeply before declining again. Almost immediately, we reach another island: Hai-aan (Hainan). We have lunch with a colonel of the Imperial Japanese Army. We are taken to a large structure which is raised five feet from the ground and is held up by six columns. On the top portion of the structure is a hall where Japanese-style tatami mats have been laid out. We rest in a corner till 4 p.m., and then continue our journey onwards.

Every minute spent between 4 and 5 p.m. will remain etched in my memory forever.

We leave Hai-aan. In the distance, the waves of the Pacific Ocean dance under a shimmering sun. Floating under the plane is another ocean—one of dense, impenetrable clouds. It feels as though we are flying over fields of white cotton.

In between these thoughts, a crew member passes me a chit which reads: 'The enemy fighter planes have spotted us. Be prepared.'

Papa and I look at each other, and smile. We tie our seatbelts firmly and remain motionless. Suddenly, there is darkness on all four sides. And I feel as though I am falling downwards through a black, endless pit. To where but hell? Then nothing. I don't know what happens next. When I open my eyes, I find I am seated the same way, still buckled to my seat. Papa and the others are sitting quietly, as though nothing has happened. I look out of the small porthole. The plane is skirting the ocean's waves.

An hour later, we reach a small island named Oryu. We step out of the plane and place our feet on solid ground. It is a wonder to still be alive, having danced with and nearly embraced death. Everyone is equally astonished.

The captain of the plane, Kimura, approaches Papa and asks him for forgiveness, his head lowered. 'Forgive me; I caused you all hardship. I was helpless. If we remained higher up, the enemy would have definitely been able to strike us. They were flying in fighter planes, and we were just in a bomber. We would have needlessly given up our lives. That's why I immediately brought the plane down to the same level as the ocean. Fortunately, because of the dense clouds, the enemy fighter planes could not see us and we escaped from their clutches.'

After saving us from a terrible death, the pilot asks for our forgiveness. This is an example of Japanese humbleness.

The small island of Oryu is absolutely desolate. You can see from one end of the island to the other. The tension in the atmosphere is palpable, though. The enemy airplanes can come any time and drop bombs on us. It will not take much to destroy us. On one part of the island, there is a single cottage with some camouflage hanging on its roof. We go inside and see a group of Japanese soldiers preparing for battle. Looking at the wireless operator, I am astonished. He is no older than eighteen or nineteen, but his innocent face is shining with excitement.

We retire for the night. Toilets are very problematic here, and I have to go quite far alone. However, there is running water in the taps, so I am able to take a French bath.[32]

Malaria is prevalent and troublesome on the island. As soon as dusk falls, the mosquitoes begin attacking us. We get into our mosquito nets and await the attack of the other Mosquitoes.

Sunday, 6 May 1945

I rise before dawn, at about 4 a.m. I stroll on grass that is soaked with the dew of the war. Hearing the youthful songs of crickets, I remember Taichu again. I remember those blooming faces who are now sleeping eternally under the Pacific Ocean along with the ships of our enemies.

7 a.m.: Departure. At 10 a.m., we reach Kampong Kung,[33] a small city on the border of Vietnam and Cambodia. This city was first under French rule, then American, and now it is under Japanese jurisdiction. We travel on a road made of red earth from the airport to the city, canopied by the branches of peepal trees on both sides. Thanks to the shade of the trees, we reach the city without sweating too much.

Kampong Kung looks like it belongs in one of Andersen's fairy tales. On either side of the road are small, colourful houses made in the French style. Their walls are webbed with ivy and studded with round French-style windows. The roofs are of all kinds of colours, aside from black. The wooden window frames of the houses are painted a matching colour. It is clear this is a French colony.

On the roads, we see Vietnamese, Cambodian and French people travelling. Their clothing is equally diverse—a Vietnamese shirt, or a European dress, or a Cambodian-style short tunic with pyjamas, and even some Japanese women in kimonos. The fields are filled with fruits, as though war hasn't left the slightest mark on the city. When I see some Japanese soldiers, I remember the war, and that I, too, am becoming a soldier. In one direction, there is the splash of French artistry and then, on the other side, are the stories of atrocities meted out by the French regime, that, till today, leave the locals palpitating with fear.

But today, there is peace with Japanese rule. I can see people looking happy. They are disciplined, but not exploited.

Surrounding Kampong Kung is a dense jungle. There is no breeze, and the city is hot. In the jungle, there is a Japanese cantonment where we eat lunch. I can barely call it a cantonment—it is more like a clearing in the jungle with an elevated floor and a thatched roof made of hay. On the floor, Japanese straw mattresses have been laid out. There is nothing beneath the floor—a large, cavernous space that lies empty and serves as a shelter during bombings. Creepers are spread on the roof as camouflage. It's such a dense jungle that it is certain the enemy will have difficulty locating this cantonment. There are several dishes served for lunch. Without eating, we will not be able to fight. The citizens of Japan have sent everything for their soldiers and are starving themselves, that's why the Imperial Japanese Army, wherever they go, are able to do amazing feats.

After an hour's rest, we depart from Kampong Kung. We reach Saigon in five minutes. We are staying in a Japanese hotel whose manager is an Indian. He asks whether I am Papa's younger sister. While I shake my head vigorously, Papa is ecstatic that people think he's still youthful. I rest in our hotel room after enjoying a long, hot shower.

***

Today, Papa tells me to wear a saree. But I don't know how to wear one. Papa then helps me put it on, taking time to drape it. I cannot walk and barely save myself from tripping many times. We eat dinner with the crew of the airplane. Wrapped in a saree, I will never be able to do any work. I even find it difficult to eat properly. I unexpectedly feel as though I have been transformed into a delicate girl.

Before slipping into my sleeping suit, I say to Papa: 'Girls should be somewhat gentle, no matter how strong they are.'

Papa rises and says: 'If you think like this, you'll never be a good soldier. There is no need for a soldier to be gentle.'

Oof, I know that tenderness will not gain us independence. Who knows why I started this aimless conversation with Papa? For freedom, even flowers need to turn into stones. But after independence, if someone is to place a flower and a stone in front of me, I will always choose the flower.

I write Ma a letter.

Tuesday, 8 May 1945

The twittering of birds awakens me today. I lie in bed, comparing the dawn of the southern countries to the dreary mornings I grew up with further north. In Japan, I had to drag myself to rise. Here, it is a thrilling dawn, trembling with life, no need for coal or a matchstick. It's an hour flooded with happiness—I can hear the song of birds and am enveloped in a balsamic-blue scent; everything to seduce the mind. One doesn't feel like lying in bed even for a minute. I get up quickly and go outside. The air is heavy with the scent of flowers. In Tokyo, the flowers have no scent, but are of beautiful shades. Here, the green leaves whisper with the wind and I lose myself in nature.

The maid comes in and informs me that it is time for breakfast. I see Papa in the distance; standing near him are some officers from the Hikari Kikan. From the green of spring to the dusty brown of khaki uniforms.

After breakfast, we go to the branch of the Azad Hind Dal that Papa helped establish. Papa gives everyone permission to salute, and I salute, but I feel somewhat embarrassed. I still have the Japanese practice of bending my head and waist when greeting others. This happens spontaneously, without thought, especially when I am wearing a frock.

Papa explains, 'Look, Japan is an independent country; so if you bend and greet there it doesn't matter. People will say you have good social skills. But here, it is a sign of submissiveness.'

'But when I salute Indians and say "Jai Hind", everyone stares. It feels as though I am a spectacle.'

'They are not used to this practice yet. You should not hesitate from doing the right thing.'

From the market, we buy three pairs of shoes to wear with our uniforms—one for Papa and two for me. Everything is very expensive here. The city is beautiful, but filled with doubt. There seems to be a lot of affectation and very little faith. We have lunch at the home of a Sindhi gentleman, Komal Sahib. A long table displays several kinds of Sindhi dishes.

I also taste mango for the first time today. Papa tells me I had tried it once when I was five in India, but I have no memory of it. The first flavour of the mango is quite bizarre, and I think there may be some kind of alcohol or tonic mixed in it. But then I bite deeper into its flesh and it transforms into something nice. I enjoy the taste, the colour, the scent, everything.

In the southern countries, I am experiencing everything quickly. At ten minutes to 3 p.m., we rush to the airport. I enter the basement and inspect our luggage. A soldier rapidly lifts it and accompanies me to the plane. We are going to fly in a training plane—fortunately without a trainee pilot, but a seasoned pilot in the cockpit! No question of falling this time. It is cold inside the plane, and we sit on the wicker chairs. At 6.30 p.m., we cross the border between Vietnam and Thailand. I look towards the earth and see water everywhere.

Papa says: 'Look, we've reached Thailand. Like Holland, the ground level of this country is lower than that of the ocean. Look at how many canals there are.'

In two hours, we reach another airport, a permanent military airbase situated thirty kilometres from Bangkok.[34] We have to wait at the airport for a while. After some time, I overhear a captain admonishing a lieutenant. First, I think he is joking because the lieutenant is also smiling. But a while later, I see him wiping away his tears with his fists. I cannot believe what I am seeing.

Papa says: 'Sometimes seniors trouble their juniors. They insult them, and when one is insulted, tears are inevitable.'

A horde of soldiers approach us. They are laughing and mocking each other. One of them asks me in broken English, 'Cigarette, have you?'

Papa's cigarette case is with me, but I feel wicked. I respond in Japanese, 'No, I don't.'

He asks, 'You know Nippon-go?'

I nod and leave.

Later, Papa comes to me. 'So why didn't you give him a cigarette?'

'Doesn't he have manners? Asking me for a cigarette.' It wouldn't have made a difference if I had given him one. Sometimes, I become quite ruthless. Perhaps more than needed…?

The car arrives, and we head towards Bangkok. We enter the city at around 8 p.m. We first go to the Hikari Kikan office and meet the chief of the area. Then we go to Oriental Hotel. We spread our arms and legs on a vast bed.

We have reached the land of the Emerald Buddha. Tomorrow, we will go to Burma—the country of Ba Maw. And then, with the words 'Chalo Delhi' on our lips, we will reach India. What must the Red Fort be like? We will meet Gandhiji and Nehruji. But, for now, Delhi is still far.

Tuesday, 15 May 1945

At 5.30 p.m., we go to the home of Shri Ishar Singh. He introduces us to his daughter, Pavitra Kaur, and his sister-in-law. Looking at her hair, I immediately think of Ma. Ma puts sindoor—the red powder—in the parting of her hair, but these people don't. I ask them why and am told that it isn't a custom among the Sikhs, but a custom in Bengal and Bihar. And so I learn another example of our diversity. They ask me to sing a Japanese song and I sing

'*Shina No Yoru*' and explain the meaning behind the words. And then, in broken Hindustani, I chat with them.

I learn a lot—Sikhism is a religion in which war is justified. Guru Nanak was its founder. And what warriors they are! They have long black hair cascading down below their waists. When we arrived, they had just washed their hair, and it fell open over their shoulders. They were playing tennis, wearing nothing but vests and underpants. I have never seen such a sight in Japan. Gosh, my short hair! My hand spontaneously goes to my bare neck.

Papa looks at me and probably understands my emotions. He asks: 'What's the matter?'

I then learn another new thing. In the Sikh religion there are five tenets. You have to retain five things starting with the letter 'k': kesh (uncut hair), kada (an iron bracelet), kanghi (a wooden comb), kripan (an iron dagger), and kaccha (underpants). Guru Nanak had pledged that till they were victorious, the Sikhs would not break these five vows. These have now become a custom.

I remember the Japanese warriors who fought during the era of Emperor Meiji. They fought to protect the Japanese dynasty. They, too, had taken a similar pledge—till they were victorious, they would not cut their beard, hair or moustache. The seeker is he who walks to his objective with perseverance.

Dinner is served in the mess of the ministers of the Azad Hind Government. Khan Sahib (D.M. Khan, one of the advisers to the Azad Hind Government) is the manager of the mess. He is quite choleric, and is always scolding the staff and servants of the mess. His roars halve the little hunger I have. Papa and Mr Sarkar continue to laugh and joke, and that's the only reason the tension reduces while we eat—else everyone's liver function would fail!

Mr Sarkar's riddle: 'The more you dig, the bigger it gets. What is it?'

Das Kaka responds: 'After dinner.'

Wednesday, 16 May 1945

I visit the Indian Independence League today. While waiting for Papa, I chat in Hindi and Japanese with Mr Sarkar. We return home in the afternoon. We are resting after lunch when Major Rao visits. I learn a lot on the topics of Dravidianism and Aryanism. I also share my knowledge of Japanese tribal groups—the Ainu and the Ezo.

Papa goes to meet Netaji at 3 p.m. When he returns, he is humming. He goes to our room to change his clothes. I see that he has worn a suit and is singing while knotting his tie. All questions are forbidden. He returns after an hour with a Bengali gentleman who has come from Burma and is a close friend of his. We chat in Bengali. Then I sing whatever Bengali songs I know. We all sing *'Dhana dhanya pushpe bhara'* and *'Urdha gagane'* together.

Today, I have the opportunity to analyse the character traits of two individuals: Major Rao, a follower of etiquette, is a philosopher. The Bengali gentleman, on the other hand, is cheerful and gregarious, the type who sits cross-legged on a sofa. His eyes are as sharp as arrows, but when he sings, his eyes soften and become dewy.

Thursday, 17 May 1945

Today, we must leave our two-storeyed house on Wireless Road[35] and shift to Panditji's home. Pandit Raghunath Sharma is the president of the IIL in Thailand. Four members of the INA will now be staying in the house on Wireless Road. Panditji also has a house within the city, but we will stay in the house outside the city. Papa will stay with Netaji. I have been given a small room, which has glass walls on three sides and a built-in cupboard on one side. Close by is Panditji and Mataji's room.[36] The home is full of women and children. This is not only Panditji's home, but also that of his two brothers. The children are all sweet—especially Raj Kumari who is an absolute doll. There is a lot of activity in the home at all times.

In the evening, Panditji comes into the courtyard, and all the women immediately retreat indoors. Mataji also lowers the cloth covering her head. I ask why, and Panditji begins laughing. I ask Papa later, and he, too, starts laughing. No one tells me anything. They only laugh. I'll ask Mataji later.

After lunch, we go to meet Netaji. There are many people seated in the veranda; I assume they are waiting to meet him. Papa tells me I can go meet Netaji inside the room. I peek inside and see Netaji sitting quietly on a sofa in the corner, looking somewhat worried.

I enter the room and say, 'Jai Hind!'

He looks at me and asks: 'You have come here to fight? You want to fight, correct?'

'Yes, Sir.'

He continues: 'Alright, get enlisted in the Rani of Jhansi Regiment.'

After saying this, he again looks grave and worried. I can understand; he has been forced to return from Burma, despite being so close to Imphal. I spot an unfastened button on his coat's collar. Usually perfectly attired, it is rare to see Netaji scattered and unsettled. But today, he looks somewhat defeated and discouraged.

***

I go to the Rani of Jhansi Camp and meet a group of sisters who have just returned from Burma. They are exhausted, but still inspired. They are impatient to reach Imphal. I learn that the

INA officers wanted to send Netaji back by air for his security, but he refused outright.

He said, 'When my heroines are walking through the jungles, then why should I fly and reach in an instant? I will go with them.'

The girls faced many difficulties and obstacles during their journey. To escape the enemy's target, they often had to leave their truck and enter the thick jungle, camouflaging themselves with the foliage that surrounded them. Even then, the enemy airplanes spotted them. There was frequent strafing—fighter planes would descend, approach as close as possible, and then spray them with machine-gun bullets. Our INA brothers always tried to protect their sisters, but still, some girls succumbed to the fate of death.

Their tales of suffering are unimaginable—they had to be without water for five days; some Ranis were suffering from malaria, yet they continued to walk; halfway through their journey their truck was burnt down. A jeep was sent from Bangkok, which brought back the women suffering from diseases. Then a truck was sent in which the remaining girls returned, along with Netaji. Netaji's order was simple—till there is an INA brother, no sister should face any kind of harm.

As Ranis, our dreams differed—we wished to lose our lives so that our brothers could live forever.

The deaths of some Ranis saddened Netaji greatly. He gave an order to Captain Janaki Bai: 'Those who have survived should be looked after appropriately. We must not lose a single girl now.'

In Imphal, over the hills of Manipur, the British and Americans are doing their best to make the Japanese and Azad Hind forces surrender. On the microphone, they are loudly announcing: 'Come this side. You'll reach home quickly. There's lots of food. Why do you want to die of hunger and thirst over there? Your mother and your sister are crying for you; your wife and your children are crying for you! Come, come!'

As though our brave brothers will ever bow down. We have vowed to win, vowed to go to Delhi and watch the tricolour flag fly free over the Red Fort. We can no longer remain enslaved. Those Azad Hind officers and soldiers who were part of the British Army know the modus operandi of the enemy very well. They can never be fooled.

Papa drops me off at the camp, where I meet a Bengali girl by the name of Pratima Dasgupta. Papa says he will come back for me later. As I wait for him, night falls and I become sleepy. I fall asleep in Captain Janaki Bai's room. Papa arrives at around 11 p.m. and we both return to Panditji's house. We are made to drink a full glass of milk before we go to sleep.

Friday, 18 May 1945

I am learning Hindi from Panditji. He is teaching me so lovingly that I feel like he is my father, too.

'Don't call me Panditji,' he says. 'Everyone here calls me Pitaji.'

Father. Since then I've started calling him Pitaji, but I never say the words in front of Papa. He may not like it. After lunch, we go to Netaji's house.

Wednesday, 30 May 1945

I am a member of the RJR from today. But I am conflicted—I have been living in close proximity to Panditji's family for so many days that I am now saddened to leave the children. Life here is rustic—cows, goats, chickens and so on are all members of the family. You can feel the strong bonds that hold a joint family together. I had heard about this aspect of Indian society from Ma, but this is the first time I have experienced it. I notice that the father's role is most prominent—every word of Panditji's becomes a rule for the family. Behind Panditji's firmness lies infinite love. Mataji's each action is also filled with tender love and care. For example, I enjoy snacking rather than eating full meals, and she worries about this. Whenever I meet her, she gives me titbits to eat.

I had to reach the camp in the morning, but Papa got late returning from the League, and so I could only reach in the evening.

It is now nine at night, and I am sitting on my mattress, writing. I am in a large hall of the Rani of Jhansi Camp. There is no bed here. We place a sheet on a mattress and sleep: after all, this is military life. Compared to life in Tokyo, this is comfort beyond belief. When I arrived this evening with Papa, all the girls of the camp came to greet me. Papa handed me over to Captain Janaki Bai and left. I went for a bath, and when I returned, Pratima Dasgupta took care of me. She took out one of her sarees, helped me wear it and then brushed my hair. Everyone stared in my direction.

Thursday, 31 May 1945

Netaji arrives at 7.30 a.m. All the girls sit in the hall with their legs crossed, but I sit on my knees in Japanese style. Netaji's speech is in Hindustani, which I find quite difficult to understand. He uses the word 'chunaanch' several times which I don't know the meaning of. I understand the gist of what he is saying and later ask another girl to explain.

There is a sadness in Netaji's voice today. Why shouldn't there be? With such courage, he had raised the morale and courage of others, marching on despite many obstacles. Victory came within a few feet before retreating, a tide under the spell of the moon. A little more time, a few more weeks without rains, and the INA would have won and crossed the border into India. But the monsoons had sided with the British. Netaji's heart is not made of stone. His mind is filled with sadness and despair. Yet, he has given us, the daughters of Free India, the strength to march on. He uses an example from the Bhagavad Gita: death, loss, victory, disease, glory—everything is a part of the world. But those who walk on the path of truth must march on to destroy evil, even if it means sacrificing one's life.

After the speech, the bell rings for breakfast. The dining hall is at a short distance from our building. We serve ourselves on plates and sit wherever we can find space.

Sunday, 3 June 1945

It's been three days since I have met Papa. Why hasn't he come? Normally, I would be concerned, but I am quite preoccupied learning my new daily routine. The first part of the training causes me no difficulties—walking in step or abiding by the orders of the captain is easy for me. I've been doing this since my school days. I tell Captain Janaki that I should be taught how to use a rifle at the earliest.

I spend all evening with Shanti Bhowmick. I am having a lot of fun talking in Bengali. We both chat intensely, talking about our mothers. We then receive some bad news. Two Ranis have died in the treacherous jungles between Burma and Thailand. One Rani was the mother of two children; her husband is also a member of the INA, fighting in Burma. She was returning from Burma to be with her children when she succumbed to malaria and typhoid. The other Rani became the target of a machine gun. Battered and bruised, they must have fallen with dreams of Free India in their eyes. Our country doesn't have one Rani Lakshmi Bai, but a countless number. This is the land of Goddess Durga.

The path from Rangoon to Moulmein is treacherous and distressful under normal circumstances. But, in the dark of the night, it is something else entirely. You cannot see even an inch in front of your eyes. It's difficult to stay safe from dangerous insects and animals. Whispering 'Jai Hind' under their breaths, the soldiers marched ahead, their lives in the palms of their hands. Paying tribute to these martyrs, we promise that we will exorcise the demons that have enslaved us.

Wednesday, 6 June 1945

Papa arrives. He notices that I have become thin and dark in only six days; he looks sad. Dinner is at Mr Thaivala's home. We do not take a car, but a san lun, which is a three-wheeler. It's a Chinese word, the equivalent of a sumaro in Japanese. What a strange language Thai is! Although people nearby are Mongoloid, the Thais sometimes say 'l' for 'r' and sometimes 'r' for 'l'. There are two types of rickshaws—one is called a jin rickshaw, which is pulled by a man, and the other is a san lun rickshaw.

When Thailand was known as Siam, Mr Thaivala kept his name as 'Siamvala', meaning 'from Siam', and when it changed, he changed his name to Thaivala. Seems like when it changes back to Siam, he may change his name again.

The word 'Thai' means peace. 'Siam', on the other hand, is the name of a race. The Siam race used to rule over a small piece of land in southern China. The Chinese king in Canton continually exploited and attacked the Siamese; they could no longer bear these attacks and atrocities, and they fled southwards. They started living in northern Thailand and gradually their kingdom spread south.

The spread of the Buddhist religion is very interesting. I have heard that there were wars between kingdoms of southern

India. The defeated king would often flee to southern Burma or Thailand with his companions, crossing the ocean on a ferry. This is how the Buddhist religion spread. The foundations of Indian culture in Thailand originated in a location called Si Thep (Shiv Dev), and then Indian-style rule was established in Ayutthaya (Ayodhya). Possibly, the fleeing dynasties of southern India influenced the Siamese race via the Mahabharata and the Ramayana. The Siamese were seeking peace after years of Chinese exploitation, and they may have found it in 'Ram Rajya', or the kingdom of Ram, after befriending the Indians in exile. The Siamese kings have ancient names, similar to the ones found in the Puranas, such as Narsimhan Bhumipala, Ram, and so on. The style of dressing is also similar to that found in India—a pha chung hang, which is a type of dhoti or lower-body wrap, accompanied by a tunic. The king and priests of Siam wear this dress till today.

We finish dinner at Mr Thaivala's place and a political debate begins. I remain seated with the women upstairs. Then I return to the camp.

When leaving, Papa says to me in a heavy tone: 'I may leave Bangkok in a few weeks. I don't know when I will return. Take care of your health and don't forget the things Ma has told you.'

Seeing Papa emotional makes me cry. But I am my father's daughter. I will not be defeated. I say, 'Jai Hind' and he leaves.

When I return to my room, the Ranis are busy discussing going to Singapore. Even before their training is complete, they will be sent there. They will all receive the rank of sub lieutenant.

As a part of training at camp, we learn both firing and nursing. Because of the current crisis, training now happens over fewer days. After one month's heavy training, we will be eligible to go to war.

I lie down and listen to the chatter of my compatriots, writing what I hear. When I listen with interest, my hand stops moving. Some women are newly married, and both husband and wife are soldiers of the INA. The women show each other their letters and joke, saying things which seem strange while we are leading military lives. At first, I feel it is inappropriate, but then, after giving it some thought, I understand. When soldiers leave their wives, children and lovers, they release their emotions by sharing their thoughts with their friends. This doesn't mean they are less dutiful or love their country any less.

I recall an incident with Ram Singh. How restless he is to talk to me. He isn't even embarrassed. No matter how far I go, he does not leave my side. Anyway, he won't dare come here. Sometimes I feel pity and think if he comes again I will talk to him properly. However, when I see him, all my mercy vanishes. These are pointless thoughts. The only work I have is to serve the nation. I fall asleep asking for Ma, Papa and Netaji's forgiveness.

Saturday, 9 June 1945

I am learning Hindi from Lieutenant Singh. He has given me a book in Hindi named *Kalavati*. I have to read it and write about it. It is difficult, but I have made a start. Papa visits today, and I introduce him to Lieutenant Singh.

Later, I go with Papa to the League. I chat with Mr Sarkar in Japanese. We have lunch with a Gurkha family. The Gurkhas eat in a manner similar to the Japanese—on the floor with a small table in front of them. On the way back, on the san lun, I tell Papa about camp life. The food is fine and so is the training, but some girls fight a lot. When they quarrel so much with each other, how will they face the enemy?

Papa laughs and asks: 'Do you fight or not? You might as well learn.'

I jerk back. 'Hah, why should I learn!'

When we return to camp, I inform the girls that I have complained to Papa about their quarrelsome behaviour. They all raise their voices and protest: 'Why did you squeal on us? You're very cunning.'

I respond: 'Then why do you all fight? Especially on such insignificant matters? Don't fight and I won't say anything.'

The siren is blaring. We will have to go into the trenches again.

A few days later

Panditji comes to the camp with his family; we chat for a bit and then he goes to do his work.

We are taught how to fire rifles for the first time today. They are extremely heavy, and it's very difficult to lift the rifle and then quickly drop it, the way everyone else does. But it is a lot of fun shooting it. Let's see when I get the chance to shoot our enemies.

It has rained all afternoon, and I spend the time practising my written Hindi. In the evening, Emily and Pauline dance. I contribute by teaching everyone the Russian polka dance. Before sleeping, I go meet Captain Janaki Bai. We speak briefly in broken English.

I ask her, 'Captain Sahib, when will I get the opportunity to go to the front?'

She informs me I can go to Burma as soon as my training is over. However, first I must learn to give orders. Then I must learn military statistics and guerrilla warfare.

She says: 'You need to become an officer. An officer's work is not simply giving orders—the orders need to be given appropriately, and one must ensure that they are obeyed at once. Officers whose orders are violated are unworthy. It is the duty of the soldier to obey orders, but sometimes the officer's orders are inappropriate and irrational. Here, the soldier doesn't become a rebel, but an adversary. It is for this reason that we officers need to give orders with wisdom and in the correct spirit.'

I hear her out and say 'Jai Hind' and return to my room. I do not salute since I am not wearing a cap on my head. At the moment, I am nothing—I do not even have the qualities of a good soldier. I do not need to go to the front just to be a target of the enemy. Nor do I want to risk the lives of our platoon's soldiers needlessly. I dream of becoming a worthy officer. With this hope, I finish this page.

Wednesday, 13 June 1945

Today, we walk to a clearing in the jungle outside Bangkok city limits. There are clumps of thorny bushes here and there, and we learn how to camouflage ourselves. We tear braided vines from the jungle foliage and cover ourselves from our heads to our knees. We then hide behind some bushy mounds and practise guerrilla war.

Our objective is to find the location of our enemy—in this case, Pratima's platoon hidden somewhere in the jungle—and then attack them. Rasammah, the younger sister of one of our seniors, Ponnammah, serves as our group leader;[37] we sometimes hide behind her and sometimes race ahead. This is how we make progress. About two hours later, we locate the enemy—at one end of the jungle we spot a bunch of vines moving in an extraordinary manner. We freeze and observe the behaviour of the vines for a while. What's even more fun is that the vines stop moving as soon as we spot them.

Suddenly, Rasammah gives us the order to attack and we shout, 'Jai Hind—Chalo Dilli!' We attack the vines and discover our well-equipped enemy. The vines fall to the ground with cries of defeat and raised hands. We are so enthused that we almost injure them with the muzzles of our rifles—but halt in the nick of time due to Rasammah's timely order. We shout and they drop leafy camouflage and show themselves. Who is it? Shanti? Arre wah. I am laughing, gasping, ready to tear her apart.

'You think I'm an angrez, or what?' she yelps. 'You nearly broke my hands and legs!'

'When Rasammah said to fight, why didn't you? I've let you go this time. In a battle, you must continue fighting even if you're injured. I won't spare you next time.'

But the mock war hasn't yet finished. Some members of Pratima's platoon spot us talking and slowly creep behind us. Suddenly, the enemy party orders an attack and catches us unawares. Shanti deceived us. She chatted with us and trapped us with her conversation. Our mission was to capture the mound—and, at that moment, Shanti's platoon climbed the mound victoriously. We had thought that we were very smart, as though our triumph was inevitable. And the enemy had the perfect occasion to defeat us.

At 5 p.m., there is a parade. The captain continuously scolds me today, demanding that I shout louder. I am shouting at the top of my voice, to the best of my abilities, but not having the habit of talking loudly makes my voice break.

Friday, 15 June 1945

We spend the entire day in the jungle, learning how to use a rifle and a bayonet. Effigies of Churchill and Roosevelt have been made with sacks. We have to pierce the effigy's neck with the tips of our bayonets. We take ten steps forward and on the eleventh step we shout 'Jai Hind' and pierce the effigy. When the bayonet perfectly targets the effigy's artery, we jump with joy. I firmly believe I can now kill the enemy without hesitation. Whenever I think of killing the enemy, I become restless. I can feel my blood boil within me. I wish there were some goras here itself, so that I could pierce their necks with the tip of my bayonet. Anyway, patience is a sign of endurance. One more month in this camp to thrash myself into becoming strong. And then we will cross the Irrawaddy river and march towards Imphal.

* * *

Twilight. Shanti and I are chatting near the lake; the evening passes by us, a cool breeze blowing from the south, and we get lost in the sea of our imagination. I feel embarrassed writing this in my diary, but if I don't write it down, I know my soul will never find peace. I can only share such things with Ma or my diary. Shanti starts it; she teases me by talking about her fiancé—how they will meet in India, how they will live in Calcutta. He has gone to Japan to become a pilot. I've heard it many times before. That's why I am not paying attention and my mind wanders. I wonder—will the same thing happen to me at some point? Will someone use the words 'let's meet in Free India' with me? Suddenly, Tsutomu's face flashes before my eyes. He has told me to keep on fighting. In the meantime, he, too, will go to war. Indians and Japanese fighting together and dying together. Yes, we will meet in heaven. Tsutomu is a decent boy. We are companions—in war.

Even then, in my imagination, a brave man repeatedly arrives in uniform, and like Papa and Netaji, he also laughs and wrestles difficulties with ease. Dilli abhi door hai. Delhi is still far. I am extremely ashamed today. From the desire to kill the enemy with the tip of my bayonet to abhorrent thoughts like these? Where have they fallen from? With emotions mixed with shame and anger, we leave the pleasant lakeside environment and return to our platoon.

In college, I had read poets of the Romantic period, who had left worldliness for nature. I, in the opposite manner, have run away from both nature and worldliness. The beauty and romanticism I see in rifles, uniforms and news of war far exceeds what I see in nature or the world. Joan of Arc probably felt the same way; there's nothing more beautiful than the motherland. The Rani of Jhansi, Lakshmi Bai, probably had the same inspiration—a country of one's own.

* * *

The girls gather in small groups here and there, some dressed in sarees, some in frocks and some in sarongs. We sing songs and dance after dinner. I teach Sushma and Shanti a traditional dance from Mallorca and then show everyone a Japanese dance. I don't have a Japanese fan, so I fashion one out of a newspaper. We speak with Captain Janaki Bai in broken English for a long time. Then everyone gathers together and sings '*Kadam kadam barhaye ja*'.

As I enter the captain's room, she turns to me. 'Why, Asha, how did you like today's training?'

'Captain Sahib, I will definitely be able to destroy the enemy now.'

She laughs and says: 'Seems like you've become truly mad. Arre baba, don't charge and fire at your brothers by accident, thinking they are the enemy!'

I dim my fiery spirit, and say: 'A mistake like that will never happen. But please send me to Burma quickly. I do not enjoy this relaxing life.'

Ma and my siblings are living in Tokyo without basic necessities. Rice, milk, fruit, everything becomes difficult to swallow when I think of them. After all, I've come here to fight for the country.

Captain Janaki Bai becomes grim and says: 'Asha, you are still serving the nation here. Is going into the battlefield and recklessly shooting bullets the only form of serving the nation? If you think this way, then these are incorrect ideas. Stay in the camp and complete your training. You need to make yourself strong and then you will triumph over any obstacle, otherwise quietly sitting at home may be a better option for you. You need to make yourself a worthy officer; this is your duty; this is how you will serve the nation. Now sleep. Have you finished your milk? Tomorrow, we need to go into the jungle at dawn. We will have mock guerrilla wars and then, in the evening, you will learn how to drive a jeep.'

I stand tall and say, 'Jai Hind.'

Saturday, 16 June 1945

Today, I have reached a new level of exhaustion. But I want to loudly announce that I fired a machine gun! It makes a deafening *phat-phat-phat* sound that turns the entire environment into an illusionary battlefield. The earth trembles and the air vibrates. I see the enemy's face in each blade of grass, each leaf. I enjoy myself. How does this violence enter our minds? Turning its head to the blue sky, the machine gun looks exactly like a crocodile ready to swallow its prey.

A brother from the Indian National Army teaches us how to use the machine gun. He explains things in rapid English, and, after a while, notices I have understood nothing. He then tries explaining in Hindi, but I find Hindi difficult, too. Looking at his hands, I learn how to use the gun, but cannot grasp the technicalities. I voice my difficulties to my captain, and she pats my back and says, 'Doesn't matter.' She then returns to her work. Unconvinced, I share my handicap with Pratima. She tells me to ask the Hindi teacher to explain.

In the evening, we have our Hindi class. I can tell the lieutenant's mood is off. He is speaking curtly. Pratima shifts from her seat and leaves the room. Shanti laughs and he gets angrier. I ask him to explain the workings of a machine gun. He immediately lights up and begins talking about each aspect of the gun—from its fabrication to its use. There are many kinds of teachers—from learned professors to kindergarten teachers. Even a beggar can be a brilliant teacher if he can ease the curiosity of an eager mind.

Sunday, 17 June 1945

Papa arrives. After PT (physical training), we go to the market, browsing briefly before going to Panditji's house. There are several types of Punjabi dishes laid on the table. Mataji says: 'Asha rani, today I will feed you makki ki roti.' I smile and agree, even though my insides flutter like the flame of a lamp. These people are Vaishnavas—they don't even eat onions. But a roti made of flies? I wonder: are these people actually so barbaric? It can't be.

Then Panditji stands in the middle of the courtyard and announces with a grin: 'Look, this Japanese girl doesn't understand the difference between makkhi and makki. She can't tell the difference between "k" and "kh".' Everyone bursts into giggles. He then explains it himself. 'Beti, in Punjabi, we call corn makki. You mistook it for makkhi, meaning flies. How can you even think we eat flies?'

I smile, turning red in embarrassment, and then eagerly await the Punjabi roti. While the roti is tasty, I don't think it really compares to bread or pastry. Papa's servant is also with us. Whenever he comes near me, he speaks in Japanese. I laugh at his accent. Papa asks me what is there to laugh at, while laughing himself.

After lunch, we hear a record of Hindi songs and then go to Hasan Kaka's house. His beard, which used to irritate me, has been shaved. After many days, we receive a letter from Satya Kaka; it has come from Shonan. We reply immediately.

When I return to camp in the evening, I go for my Hindi classes. Pratima and the lieutenant are still grouchy. They both want to talk, but embarrassment prevents them. The people witnessing their discomfort are having fun. Pratima has forbidden all of us from talking to the lieutenant or taking Hindi classes. What a disaster this is; they've fought and we can no longer learn Hindi?

Monday, 18 June 1945

Today, there is a separate session for officer training. I am new, and so am instructed to stand in the queue of soldiers. These new soldiers don't even know how to march in step or stand at attention. I don't enjoy being in this group at all. I don't know why the captain has put me here; is it her ignorance or some kind of policy? In the evening, I complain to her, but she just smiles. Anyway, I am a soldier. I have to obey the orders of an officer. The captain's silence seems to be helplessness to me. I even told her I've been doing PT and physical exercise since my childhood—standing in a line and marching is very easy for me. Some of the new soldiers in the line have come from rural areas, villages near Gorakhpur; they are unschooled and have never exercised. Walking or marching with them is impossible for me.

Tuesday, 19 June 1945

Today, we do not have our Hindi class. We all think of Pratima as our elder sister, and we must abide by her wishes. But spending the evening without purpose is an issue. I can't talk to anyone for very long; there aren't any books to read. I am angry with the incident in the morning and become very bored by the evening. I am marching with the new girls when the captain comes, observes us silently, and then leaves. She then gives us the orders of 'ruk ja' and 'aaram kar'. Halt and rest. She goes to speak to the lieutenant.

The lieutenant then asks me to make the team march. There is no end to my happiness. At my orders, the team becomes sweaty and tired. Like bullets, orders leave my mouth: 'Aage barh! Dayein murh! rukh ja!' March forward! Turn right! Halt! And then immediately: 'Aage barh! Peeche murh!' March forward! Turn around! It goes on. At the end, I make the new recruits salute. A beautiful salute by patriots! In their hearts, they wish to erase themselves for their country, but they have grown up within walls. They have not yet escaped the bondages of shame and hesitation. Yes, they may chatter and joke freely with their friends, but under an open sky, with strangers eyeing them, they hesitate to even lift their hands or raise their heads. They hesitate to run. Anyway, who am I to criticize these women? I always feel shy talking to others.

After training, we rest in the camp for a while. Rasammah beckons me, and I see a Japanese gentleman has arrived with his family. They have come to chat with me in Japanese. I ask the children their names, but they are too shy to respond. Then the Japanese lieutenant showers me with questions. Where is your home in Japan? Which school and college did you study in? What Japanese food do you like to eat? You must miss your mother and so on. His wife sits quietly, looking like a true Japanese wife. It's probably better to say 'eastern' than Japanese. I can see all the positive things of an ideal woman in her—good-natured, silent, forgiving, tolerant, obedient, and so on. In my opinion, it's not obedience but stupidity! The Japanese woman I see today has made herself inferior and lifeless. When I ask her a question, she curiously looks toward her husband. She should have answered at least once herself. The only thing she says, fearfully, is that she will bring some Japanese food for me soon. I thank her in advance.

In the evening, Papa arrives with lots of fruits. He shares them all, and we eat them happily.

Wednesday, 20 June 1945

The captain comes to know that we are not going for our Hindi classes and admonishes us. When I go to the Hindi class that evening, I see Pratima and the lieutenant gossiping furiously. If they had to be friends, why deprive us of our classes for two days? After class, Shanti and I go sit near the pond. Everyone criticizes Pratima. She thinks of herself as someone older than us, but does what she pleases. We then go for dinner—prawn curry and rice. But so spicy!

Before sleeping, the captain calls Shanti Bhowmick. Shanti and her sister, Anjuli, return to the room in tears. Their father has suddenly died. Overcome with grief, the two girls howl. The news is truly devastating. But their sorrow throws me into an ocean of thoughts—I have heard that mourning loudly is a Chinese custom. When someone dies, the Chinese call an outsider to cry loudly in support of the grieving family. The hope is that their cries of sorrow will not just reach God's ears above but spread in all four directions. It's bizarre. In Japan, I have never seen or heard such a custom. According to Japanese custom, life, death and all other events—big or small—are a game of nature. Man is a toy in the hands of nature and its elements. That's why the Japanese remain silent and can notice obscure things.

Thursday, 21 June 1945

Papa visits the camp, but does not meet me. He drops off fruits and so on, and then leaves.

We go to hear General Bhonsle's speech at Bangkok General Library. General Bhonsle describes the true state of the war: the soldiers of the INA want to go to Imphal; they cannot bear to remain here. On this the General Sahib says: 'Once the rain stops, we will march forward. The situation right now is quite delicate. It is not possible to cross the Irrawaddy river. We must wait here for some more days. Till then, focus on your physical fitness so that you do not tire out on the long road.'

Mr Thakur Singh follows the general with a rousing speech. Every word of his carries the force to destroy the enemy. His thunderous voice makes our blood boil. His speech is full of self-belief, self-strength and a bit of ego. Perhaps without this proud egoism, it is impossible to complete such great work.

When I first came south, I assumed the Japanese love for their nation was supreme. My thoughts were full of Japanese national pride, willpower, beauty and greatness. I did not see any great love for the nation in the Indians I had met in Japan. Sacrifice—which is an intrinsic part of any great love—was not visible. It felt as though most people had joined national organizations for their own prestige and status. Over the last many months, I have come to the realization that Indian patriotism is also great.

Sacrifice is not only a part of patriotism but is a quality of our whole being. I used to think—we Indians fear fighting, fear dying. We take the name of peace and non-violence. If someone slaps us, we stay silent. Didn't Mahatma Gandhi teach us to be peaceful? That we can achieve our goals through willpower? But it was Netaji who said, yes, Gandhiji's sayings are true—when someone slaps you, show him the other cheek. But, Netaji continued, it was

Walking in the snowy streets of Kobe, 1929.

Growing up in Kobe before the war: With my class teacher Mr Maeda (left) and the principal (right) of Uozaki National Elementary School.

Papa and Ma established the India Lodge in Kobe to provide shelter for young Indian students, merchants and nationalists.

Postcard of the Indo-Japanese Friendship Association formed by Papa to publicize India's independence struggle in Japan.

THE INDIAN NATIONAL CONGRESS, CABINET.

PRESIDENT
RAJENDRA PRASAD

TREASURER
JAMNA LAL BAJAJ

GENERAL SECRETARIES
JAWAHARLAL NEHRU, DR. SYED MAHMOOD, & J. B. KIRPALANI.

COMMITTEE

SARDAR VALLABHBHAI PATEL
MRS. SAROJINI NAIDU
MOULANA ABUL KALAMAZAD
MR. C. RAJAGOPAL ACHARIAR
DR. PATTABHI SITARAMAYA
MR. JAIRAMDAS DOULATBAM
DR. M. A. ANSARI
SARDAR SARDUL SINGH
KHAN ABDUL GAFFAR KHAN
MR. GANGADHARRAO DESHPANDE

JUBILEE BANQUET IN KOBE.

WORKING COUNCIL OF THE INDIAN NATIONAL CONGRESS COMMITTEE OF JAPAN

PRESIDENT
A. M. SAHAY

TREASURER
K. MANAMAL

SECRETARIES
D. N. DAS, D. J. SHAH

COMMITEE
G. B. KOTAK, D. N. KAPOOR & J. D. KOTHARI

Celebrating the Golden Jubilee of the Indian National Congress in Kobe in 1935.

The 1935 souvenir cover of *Voice of India*.

Papa travelled widely across Asia, spreading the message of India's struggle for freedom. Here he is in Manchuria in 1935.

As a young schoolgirl in Tokyo. We moved from Kobe to Tokyo so that Papa could stay in touch with prominent political leaders and extend his nationalistic activities.

My German-Japanese friend Hanako-san and I pose with our dolls in Ogikubo, Tokyo, accompanied by Papa and Hanako's mother, Fujji auntie.

With our Tokyo neighbours, the Ogatas, on New Year's Day, 1941. Seated left to right: Satya Kaka, Papa, Baby, Ma, Ashok and Obasan. Tulu and I are standing behind Papa and Ma.

Saluting freedom: Ma surrounded by her children Ashok, Baby, Tulu, and me (standing). The Swaraj tricolour flag with the charkha emblem hangs behind us in our Tokyo living room.

Ma and I with Netaji Subhas Chandra Bose at Imperial Hotel during his first visit to Tokyo in 1943.

Netaji with members of the Indian community in Japan. Seated in the front row are Papa (second from the left) and Ma (left of Netaji), while Tulu and I are standing in the third row above Papa.

The cabinet of Netaji's Azad Hind Government was announced on October 21, 1943.

Bottom row left to right: Maj. Gen. A.C. Chatterji, Maj. Gen. J.K. Bhonsle, Netaji Subhas Chandra Bose, Lt Col. Dr Lakshmi Sahgal, Anand Mohan Sahay, S.A. Ayer.

Middle row from left to right: Maj. Gen. (Dr) A.D. Loganathan, Col. Ehsan Qadir, Maj. Gen. N.S. Bhagat, Maj. Gen. Mohammed Zaman Kiani, Maj. Gen. Aziz Ahmad Khan, Maj. Gen. Shah Nawaz Khan, Col. Gulzara Singh.

Top row left to right: Debnath Das, (second and third not known), A. Yellappa, Sardar Ishar Singh Narula.

The Greater East Asia Conference in Tokyo in November 1943 chaired by Japanese Prime Minister Gen. Hideki Tojo. Netaji Subhas Chandra Bose, Head of the Provisional Government of Free India, was invited as an observer. He was accompanied by Papa (standing immediately behind Netaji, extreme right), Gen. J.K. Bhonsle, Col. Dr D.S. Raju and Col. Abid Hasan.

The leaders of the nations, seated left to right, are: President Ba Maw of Burma, Prime Minister Zhang Jinghui of Manchuria, President Wang Jingwei of China, Gen. Hideki Tojo of Japan, Prince Wan Waithayakon of Thailand, President Jose P. Laurel of the Philippines and Netaji Subhas Chandra Bose.

Papa in his INA uniform. He served in the cabinet of the Azad Hind Government as Secretary (with ministerial rank).

My uncle, Satyadev Sahay, Director of the Intelligence Bureau of the INA.

Papa accompanied Netaji Subhas Chandra Bose on several important missions. He is pictured here, on the right, arriving in Port Blair for the official handover of the Andaman Islands to the Azad Hind Government.

Netaji and Papa in the Andamans with Japanese generals, after the handover to the Azad Hind Government.

Papa (left) with Netaji at the Cellular Jail in the Andaman Islands.

Off to war! Seated in the centre in my INA uniform with my classmates of Showakojo College during my farewell ceremony in 1945. To my right is my class lecturer and to my left is my best friend Suzuki-san.

With my seniors of Showakojo College. Seated to my right is my hostel superintendent and to my left is my class lecturer.

Posing with my best friend Suzuki-san before heading off to war.

I joined the Rani of Jhansi Regiment training camp in Bangkok in early 1945, after making a perilous journey from Tokyo to Bangkok with my father. Prior to joining the training camp, I briefly met Netaji in Bangkok.

Standing with the wives of the jailers at our detention camp in Bangkok.

With Pandit Raghunath Sharma, his wife Kesra Devi Sharma and daughter Rajo (Rajkumari) in Bangkok. I stayed with the Sharmas for a year after the war, when the Rani of Jhansi Regiment was disbanded. Pandit Sharma served as the President of the Indian Independence League, Thailand, and was arrested and jailed in Pearl Hill Prison, Singapore, at the same time as Papa.

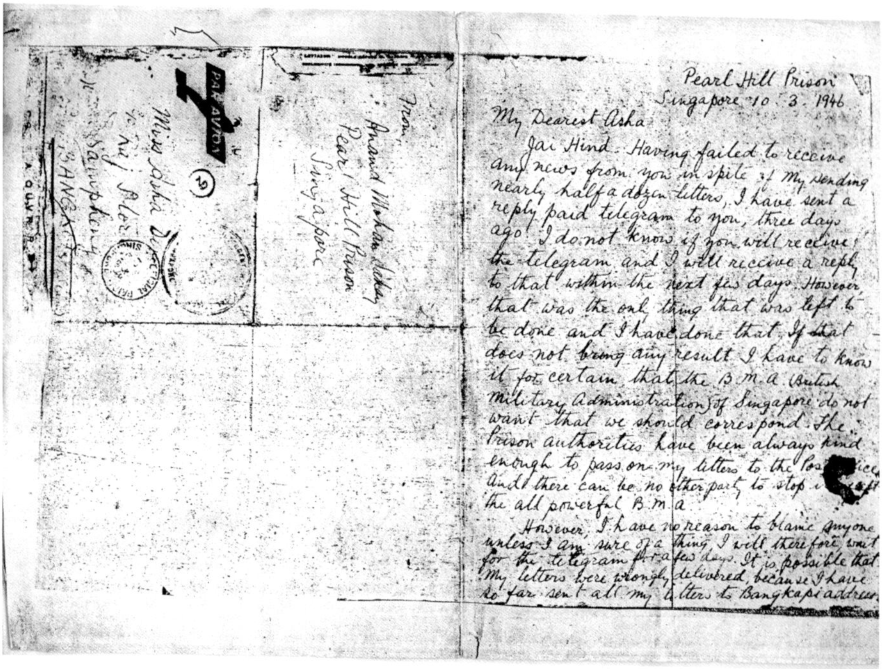

PAR AVION

Miss Asha D...
c/o Raj Store
Sampheng
BANGKOK

From:
Anand Mohan Sahay
Pearl Hill Prison
Singapore

Pearl Hill Prison
Singapore 10.3.1946

My Dearest Asha

Jai Hind. Having failed to receive any news from you in spite of my sending nearly half a dozen letters, I have sent a reply paid telegram to you, three days ago. I do not know if you will receive the telegram and I will receive a reply to that within the next few days. However that was the only thing that was left to be done and I have done that. If that does not bring any result I have to know it for certain that the B.M.A. (British Military Administration) of Singapore do not want that we should correspond. The Prison authorities have been always kind enough to pass on my letters to the Post Office. And there can be no other party to stop it except the all powerful B.M.A.

However, I have no reason to blame anyone unless I am sure of a thing, I will therefore wait for the telegram for a few days. It is possible that my letters were wrongly delivered, because I have so far sent all my letters to Bangkapi address.

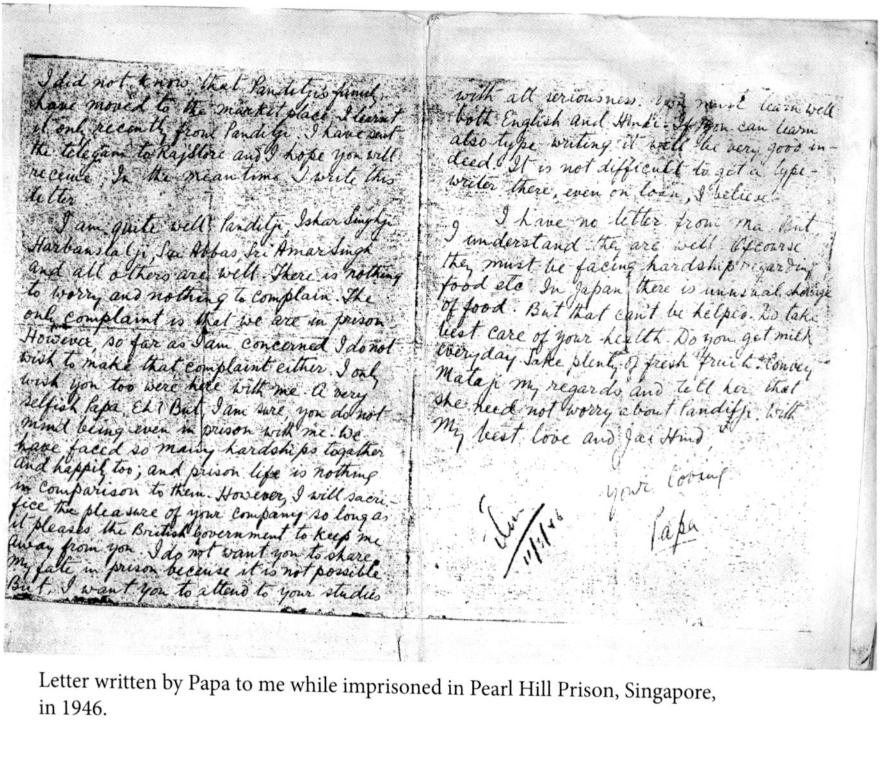

I did not know that Panditji's family have moved to the market place. I learnt it only recently from Panditji. I have sent the telegram to Rajstore and I hope you will receive. In the mean time I write this letter.

I am quite well. Panditji, Ishar Singhji, Harbanslalji, Sri Abbas, Sri Amar Singh and all others are well. There is nothing to worry and nothing to complain. The only complaint is that we are in prison. However, so far as I am concerned I do not wish to make that complaint either. I only wish you too were here with me. A very selfish Papa. Eh! But I am sure, you do not mind being even in prison with me. We have faced so many hardships together and happily too; and prison life is nothing in comparison to them. However, I will sacrifice the pleasure of your company so long as it pleases the British Government to keep me away from you. I do not want you to share my fate in prison because it is not possible. But I want you to attend to your studies with all seriousness. You must learn well both English and Hindi. If you can learn also type writing it will be very good indeed. It is not difficult to get a typewriter there, even on loan, I believe.

I have no letter from Ma. But I understand they are well. Of course they must be facing hardship regarding food etc. In Japan there is unusual shortage of food. But that can't be helped. Do take best care of your health. Do you get milk everyday? Take plenty of fresh fruit. Convey Mataji my regards and tell her that she need not worry about Panditji. With my best love and Jai Hind,

Your loving
Papa

11/3/46

Letter written by Papa to me while imprisoned in Pearl Hill Prison, Singapore, in 1946.

Reunited with Papa in Singapore in May 1946.

After being released from detention in 1946, we stayed with the Mitras in Singapore. From left to right: me, Satya Kaka, Papa, Gopal Mitra, and Lakshmi Mitra (children of Dr Mitra).

In Calcutta, on home soil: Papa, Satya Kaka and I toured India, sharing stories of the incredible sacrifices made by the soldiers the Indian National Army.

With Sheel Bhadra Yajee, President of the INA Relief Committee for repatriated INA soldiers.

Being welcomed at a school in Bhagalpur, Bihar.

Reception for us on our return to India by citizens of Calcutta 1946.

Left to right standing: Satya Kaka (third), Papa, me, Col. Mehboob Ahmad (private secretary to Netaji), Mrs Ghosh (social worker), Dhiraj Sharma (Congress secretary).

Col. Habib ur Rahman brought Netaji's ashes in an urn to our home in Tokyo in September 1946. The ashes were kept safely in our living room till they were sent to Renkoji Temple. Left to right: S.A. Ayer (Minister of Publicity & Propaganda, Azad Hind Government), Tulu, Col. Habib ur Rahman (Assistant Chief of Staff, Indian National Army), along with the family of Rama Murti (Head of the Indian Independence League, Tokyo). In the front row are Baby and Ashok.

The final journey: Ma, Satya Kaka, and my siblings in front of our home in Ogikubo shortly before returning to India in 1947. Left to right: Baby, Satya Kaka, Ma (seated), Tulu, and Ashok.

As a Seva Dal volunteer at a refugee camp in Meerut in 1947.

Secretary-General— **Anand Mohan Sahaya**

Mr, Satyadeo Sahaya,

Miss Asha Sahaya of I. N. A.

It fills us with unspeakable pleasure mixed with feeling of robust national pride to accord to you our most cordial reception and present this address of welcome on behalf of the organ.sations mentioned below.

We have a particular priviledge to celebrate this function in our own humble way as we claim you all as our own on a nearer and more intimate relationship and kinship.

HEROES of the Azad Hind Govt., We belong to a confraternity which knows no religion but the emancipation of the country from all hurdles and hindrances in the way of attainment and to the full growth and stature of its being. Brave Sons of India, the years of your stuggle from 1925 to 1946 will ever remain memorable in the history of India, on whose pages the names of you and your family will be inscribed in the letters of Gold.

SECRETARY GENERAL SAHAYA. you had been a distinguished personality in Japan from the year 1925 from your very arrival in Japan you hade made the Japanese realise that India is quite fit for her own Govt. instead of foreign rule, through press and public meetings. You had organised Japan branch of Indian National Congress and were its president all along. It was you who had organised the Indian National Association in China and flashed the Indian Political situation to the Chinese.

SAHAYAJI, the whole credit of bringing NETAJI from Germany to S. E. Asia and inducing him to take up the charge of the I, N. A. goes to you and you alone. May we be proud of the fact that you had been the only personality who had prepared ground in Japan and S. E. Asia for all these 20 years at the cost of your everything, this being the most important factor of success of I. N. A. so far.

Mr. SATYADEO SAHAYA, you brave brother of a brave hero and Miss. ASHA SAHAYA the bold and energetic daughter of the Patriot we can't forget your sacrifices and bravery for your duties which you discharged so faithfully and were said to be most trusted lieutenant of NETAJI.

VALLIANT Brethren of Behar, we hope and belive that you by your bold activities and selfless sacrifice will be able to give a free lead to India and achieve our freedom from the dirty foreign yoke.

BANDE MATRAM.

Members of :—

Calcutta,
17-6 46

Behar Association,
Behar Prabasi Chatra Sangh.
Barabazar Student Congress.

Heroes of the Azad Hind Government.

Being felicitated by President Ram Nath Kovind and former President Pranab Mukherjee in 2017. To my right is my son, Sanjay Choudhry.

also Gandhiji who said that if you trap a cat in his own home and then beat him, he will most definitely bite you. We are the cats whom the British have trapped in their own homes, to be beaten. We must bite. And become independent.

Today, Thakur Singh's speech shakes me up. I feel as though someone has put oil on the fires of my patriotism. The stories of the Battle of Imphal—a battle of courage and bravery—are heartfelt and painful. Our brothers faced countless dangers and saw a glimpse of victory. The enemy rained bullets on them from the tops of the hills. At the same time, using loudspeakers, they taunted them with memories of their families and children, the opportunity for good food and drink, psychologically affecting them. However, this attempt at distraction was unsuccessful—our brothers are not the type to get distracted by their wives and children, only the enemies are. Do they not know that Netaji's army does not have a single soldier who puts himself first? Do they not recognize the iron hearts of these heroes?

Body, mind, property—they sacrificed everything for Mother India the day they signed up with Netaji. How many flowers have withered in Manipur and Imphal, and we, the new buds, are once again getting ready to bloom. We are inspired to meet and destroy the enemy. Yes, Delhi is still far away, but the struggle for freedom has just begun. We don't know how many times we will have to see the face of loss. But our fury and hatred against the enemy is increasing. Today, helplessness forces us to return from the gates of India. We are left feeling extremely disappointed.

How must Netaji feel? In battle, victory and loss are natural, but the heart gets deeply injured. The urge to fight echoes in our heads. Losing hope is the first sign of defeat. Without hope, devotion and diligence, no effort will be successful.

Today, I am thrilled—because I understand the true meaning of worshipping one's nation.

Friday, 22 June 1945

It has been raining since the morning, but we do a parade, nonetheless. General Bhonsle positions himself for the inspection. We stand at attention, very conscious of our stance.

Monday, 25 June 1945

I go to the market today with Papa and take Pratima along with me. Our photograph is taken together. I buy a yard of green linen cloth. We then go to Parmanandji's house for lunch. The lunch is Thai—rice cooked in coconut milk. Papa has been very silent all day. Sometimes he quietly glances at me.

Tuesday, 26 June 1945

Today, we visit the Temple of the Emerald Buddha. It is said that Naresh, the king of Lanka, gifted this emerald-green statue to the Thai king. He brought the statue from Varanasi to Lanka. There is a veranda on the periphery of the temple and murals are painted on the walls depicting scenes from the Mahabharata and the Ramayana. Each person, each object is painted skilfully and soulfully.

Ma had narrated the tales of the Ramayana to us and I had even read some in Japanese. While these depictions are somewhat strange, I am forced to lower my head with reverence and appreciation. What imagination and what ability! Papa tells me it isn't just artistry that makes these works great—it is also devotion. The artists have transferred their souls into these paintings. Without devotion, without willpower, no work can be great. We will never find success in tasks where our ego and attachment are involved. Another word for devotion is belief.

Apart from belief, there is no such thing which gives us success, peace and freedom.

Papa speaks haltingly. Sometimes, he looks at me, his face creasing into sadness. There must be something. While we are on the san lun, I sing a song by Madhav Shukla for Papa:[38]

On my mother's head rests a crown,[39]
the gardens of India are green
with the flowers of Nehru, Gandhi,
Vallabhbhai, Azad and Ansari
in our laps, Subhas will be victorious.

On my mother's head rests a crown,
a cover of pleasant rain,
the country of India becomes green,
erasing the pains of our farmers,
each house with grain aplenty.

On my mother's head rests a crown,
may there be love between Hindus and Muslims,
may our brothers be affable,
may the fields of freedom see spring,
and the rule of happiness reign over India.
On my mother's head rests a crown.

* * *

I hear the sound of the siren while I'm writing. I race towards the trench near the pond. Suddenly a strange noise—*soo-dhab*—and then the sounds of bombs exploding, glass shattering. The sound of something falling.

An airplane descends and begins strafing the ground—the air explodes with dust and machine-gun fire. I get out of the trench and see war erupting around me. Lying down and crawling forward, Shanti and I reach the spot where one of our INA brothers is lying near an anti-aircraft gun, veiled in bushes. Next to him is another brother, also lying down, trying to tie a handkerchief around his arm.

'We are going to get the first-aid box,' we say.

'No, not yet. The bombing has not stopped.'

Blood drenches the handkerchief. Shanti whispers in my ear, 'Chalo, let's go get it.'

Leaving the safety of the trench, we scramble into the camp building. We race up to the area where supplies are kept and grab the first box we can find. Bombs are still falling. We go back outside and fall to the ground, crawling back to the spot where our injured brother is waiting. We tie a bandage on his arm and sigh in relief. Then we remember that we have a first-aid box in our trench too. Why did we have to go running so far away? Shanti and I collapse into giggles.

It is now 11 p.m. The bombing has halted for now. We return to our camp. One corner of the camp has been destroyed.

During the day—an excursion to see the Temple of the Emerald Buddha, and pensive conversations with Papa. And at night—the uninvited arrival of the enemy, followed by destruction and escape.

Wednesday, 27 June 1945

I go to the city today. This time not with Papa, but with the other Ranis. We go to a temple which has a full-sized statue of the Buddha reclining in a long hall. I then go with Pratima to the photographer's shop and we both get our photographs taken. Tomorrow, we will leave our camp building and shift into a building next to Panditji's house. Some girls will go to Singapore. Our commanding officer will also be leaving.

Friday, 29 June 1945

Captain Janaki Bai calls me to see her today. I hear from her that Papa has gone somewhere far. I am a soldier and so is he; I have my duties and so has he. We do not have the right to seek information about each other's activities. If Papa had to leave without meeting me, I have no right to be regretful. To be sad is natural, but, as a soldier, I can have no relationship with my emotions.

Today we are here, tomorrow there, this is the journey of life.

Still, he could have met me and then left.

June–July 1945[40]

Today, we are shifting to the new camp near Panditji's home.

We have learnt that Netaji has sent the ministers of the Azad Hind Government to various cities across Asia. Papa and Colonel Chatterji have gone to Saigon.

The British forces have again dominated Burma. Atrocities against the soldiers of the INA have begun. We know there will be no boundaries this time. It is war, after all. Netaji condemned these atrocities on the radio. He said:

> Information that has reached us from reliable sources in Burma goes to show that vindictive and brutal treatment is being meted out to officers and men of the Indian National Army who have been captured by the Anglo-Americans in Burma. As the whole world knows, the Anglo-Americans—and in particular the British—have always been in the habit of condemning Germany and

Japan for their supposed ill-treatment of Anglo-American prisoners of war. But I would now like to ask what the Anglo-Americans are themselves doing with the members of the Indian National Army who happened to fall into their hands in Burma.

Members of the Indian National Army are honest patriots and revolutionaries fighting for the freedom of their motherland. They, no doubt, fought bravely and stubbornly against the British, but they fought with clean hands and with a clear conscience. They are, therefore, entitled to decent treatment during captivity, in accordance with international usage and convention. Consequently, I appeal to my countrymen at home to take up the cause of their own prisoners of war, who fought for India's liberation and who are now receiving brutal and vindictive treatment at the hands of the British.

July 1945

I am touching this diary after almost a month.[41] I had caught a fever—malaria. Emily, my military companion, took care of me, and Major Rao provided medical aid. Panditji, Mataji, Ram Singh, and Ved Prakash[42] came to see me. An assistant with the Hikari Kikan, Hujii-san, brought a Japanese book for me, which I read lying down.

I don't know where the days have disappeared. I feel like I'm spinning in a cyclone—so many incidents in such a brief span of time. Everything has changed; it feels like we have reached the end of a long, drawn-out play. We, the actors, stand on a stage flooded in darkness. We cannot think of the past nor of the future. Without a director, we are frozen. To bring peace to my uneasy soul, I am writing today—slowly recalling the events of the last twenty-five days.

The storm began the day Papa secretively went 'somewhere' without meeting me. I found it strange, but kept my emotions aside. Soldiers don't have time to waste on pointless matters. I spent my days exactly how I would have if Papa were here.

We get continuous updates of the war—mostly disappointing news. The situation in Japan is dire; it is doubtful even a single soul will survive.

Mid-July 1945

At 4 p.m., the girls go for a tea party to a Sindhi gentleman's house. They ask me to join them, too, but I don't feel like it. They all get dressed and leave in a rush. I wash up and wear a fresh red saree gifted to me by Ma, feeling revitalized after my illness. Then I make both my bed and Emily's.

While doing this, I hear the horn of a car. I look down from the window and see Netaji's black car standing at the gate and stepping out from it is our venerable Netaji.[43] With him are General Bhonsle, Hasan Kaka, Ayer Sahib, and Habib Sahib. Panditji is also standing nearby. I race down, stand at attention, and loudly say 'Jai Hind'.

Netaji asks in a very grim voice: 'Where are the other girls?'

'They've gone for a tea party.'

'You didn't go. Why?'

'I didn't have the desire to go.'

He remains quiet for a few moments and then places a hand on my head and says softly: 'Ghabrana mat, Asha. There's nothing to worry about. Ma, Papa and everyone are all well.'

I bristle at his words. Ghabrana mat. Standing straight, I say, 'I do not worry.'

Netaji places a hand on my back, smiles and says, 'Good. Shahbash!' He pauses before saying in Bengali: 'Satir meye eyi to.'

He always speaks in Hindustani; this is the first Bengali sentence I have heard him say to me. I am truly Sati's daughter.

Netaji turns to Panditji and says: 'Sharmaji, till there is no decision, keep Asha with you.' They then converse about other things. I remain standing at attention. He then turns to me and says: 'Accha, then we will meet in the gathering this evening.' They all leave. Panditji tells me to go rest and also leaves.

How can I rest? At seven in the evening, I go to Netaji's camp. There are some officers and soldiers of the INA. Netaji tells us all to remain still.

Some officers speak resentfully. 'What about our future? The British will capture us, and then what will happen to our families? Can we not fight without Japanese strength?' And so on.

'Oof, cowards,' I hiss under my breath.

Emily, sitting nearby, shushes me: 'Chup! Let's see what happens.'

The other girls are also angry, but discipline has taught us to remain quiet. But our minds are turbulent—did these men start worrying about their families and their futures today? Why did they chant 'Netaji ki jai' and 'Jai Hind' if they didn't mean it? Damn them all.

I am feeling sympathetic towards Netaji—such a heavy burden on his head and encircled by doubt from all directions. But, on the empty canvas of his face, the same beatific smile. And these officers, thinking only of their own adversities, shooting questions like poisonous arrows—a poison that can pierce the heart of a man like Netaji, too. Can they not show their loyalty till the end? I quietly watch this scandal unfold, aghast.

Hasan Kaka, General Bhonsle and some others sit near Netaji, and try to explain the situation to the disgruntled officers. Their faces are symbols of perseverance. I can see who is willing to sacrifice everything versus those who are there for their own betterment.

Netaji gives an order to us girls—whoever's home is in Thailand is to return home and those who are left will stay in Bangkok's Sacred Heart Convent. I say I would like to stay in the convent, too. But Panditji interrupts me: 'Nahi, Netaji has a special concern for you; that's why he's entrusted you to me. From today, you can let Mataji know all your wishes—she will be your mother, too.' Panditji's loving words calm my soul.

We return to camp at 9 p.m. I sit in Netaji's car close to him. Happiness mingles with depression and my eyes become moist. I cannot believe such a great man is concerned about an insignificant child like me. I slowly wipe away the corner of my eye; however, a lone tear escapes and runs down my cheek. Netaji sees this, but remains silent. If he had said anything, it's possible that I would have sobbed.

Once we reach camp, Netaji looks at me. His face is soft with compassion. The black car leaves. Panditji and I continue to stare at the long road, which brought Netaji and then took him away again.

Little did I know that this was the last time I would see Netaji.

A few days later

Today, after several weeks, I am feeling better. I bathed with warm water and had some dal, rice and meat soup. Emily takes great care of me. Of all my friends, she alone is selfless, calm and understanding. She even wakes up at night to check on me. I never feel I am far from home with her nearby.

Now, I am back to my health. And staring at a turbulent, indifferent world. Let's see how everything unfolds…

Pandit Raghunath Sharma comes to meet us and informs us that we will be sent back to our homes, and those who cannot, or do not want to go home will be moved to a building near Panditji's house.

Within two or three days, the girls who are heading to Singapore via Malaya will leave. I will shift into the house near Panditji's with the girls heading to Burma.

I am finding it very sad to say farewell to my friends, especially Pratima Di.

Monday, 23 July 1945

We are in the building next to Panditji's house.[44] The Anglo-American forces have entered Bangkok. They have imprisoned our brothers and will send them to Singapore soon. They have forbidden the Ranis of our regiment to wear uniforms or to step out of the camp. Despite their instructions, we continue to wear our uniforms.

Wednesday, 25 July 1945

Several American soldiers enter our camp, eyes glinting like jackals. They yell, 'Hey, stop wearing your uniforms, you girls!'

Our English might be broken, but our spirits are strong. We reply, 'We will wear, don't you worry.' We then laugh. Their white faces look bitter, as though they are chewing on neem leaves. They confiscate our rifles, load them into a truck and leave.

We are imprisoned in our camp itself. Yesterday, some Indian officers of the British Army came to meet us. They respectfully called us behen, or sister. But we bristled and sparked at their words. We cannot forget that these are the people who killed our brothers; we see nothing but red.

'You are toadies of the English,' I said to one officer. 'You are our enemies.' The officer did not react. Instead, he joined his hands together and said: 'You all are true daughters of India. We are proud. Jai Hind!'

If the Japanese had imprisoned him, he too could have become an officer of the Indian National Army. He could have fought for our freedom. It wasn't in his fate to serve with Netaji.

End-July 1945

As per Netaji's instructions, Emily and four other girls will shift to Sacred Heart Convent today and I will move into Panditji's house. Panditji announces: 'From today, you are a member of this home. Do not hesitate for any matter.' Mataji and Panditji take me upstairs. I return to that small room encircled in glass.

I lay out the mats and mattresses on the floor. It is hot, and I feel extremely sleepy. I go downstairs and see Mataji making food in the kitchen. I sit there and observe her. All the children—Swaraj, Raj Kumari, Anand Swarup, Mahaveer—are sitting there. There are some others too—Panditji's younger brother's wife and their two daughters. The day slips away. My mind feels hollow.

Every day, I learn Hindi from Panditji. A brother from the INA comes and teaches us typing. Most members of the INA have been sent to Malaya and Singapore. Few remain here.

General Bhonsle and some other officers reside in the building next door. Like Papa, they too call me over to eat omelettes.

One day, I notice the building is empty. Where did they go? No one knows. One day, we hear there's been a ceasefire. Then the next, we hear that Russia has declared war. These are nothing but rumours. We have heard Netaji several times on the radio.

Hearing the inspiring tenor of his voice, we feel an urge to return to the battlefield.

Wednesday, 8 August 1945

In the evening, Anand Swarup comes to me and gently says: 'An atom bomb has fallen in Japan. Everything in the area has been burnt and destroyed.'

The news stuns me. Where else, other than Tokyo, could this bomb have fallen? I cannot say anything—my voice vanishes. A single image spins wildly in my head—that of Ma.

Seeing me standing frozen like a statue, Anand Swarup speaks. 'Please sit, sister.'

I sit. I have no recollection of what I said or did thereafter.

Friday, 10 August 1945

Black clouds shadow the world. We hear many things, but what can we believe? On 6 August, the American demons dropped an atom bomb.[45] The second followed on 9 August. They say it is a holocaust. It's possible a bomb has fallen on Tokyo, too. We can't believe what we hear on the radio any more. Demons show mercy, but these demons exhibit only unimaginable cruelty and barbarism. How wicked are they and their companions who—without hesitation—have done an act like this? We hear that even the ashes of the bomb can kill. The winds of the bomb can deform. Death comes as a breeze and freezes men, women and children in perpetuity. People with laughter on their faces now laugh forever; those with their hands raised, raise their hands forever; those with tears in their eyes continue crying forever. What a terrible state it is.

Netaji instructed us to be happy and fearless before leaving. Even Netaji must have shivered hearing this monstrous tale. We, the soldiers of the INA, are believers in violence, but we haven't lost our humanity—unlike the American demons.

Let's see what else we hear.

Tuesday, 14 August 1945

Netaji's statement has been broadcast from Shonan.

Wednesday, 15 August 1945

Radio Tokyo announces the surrender of Japan. Emperor Hirohito addresses his subjects directly for the first time in history. He says: 'I do not want the red symbol of Nippon to be erased from the map of the world. While we dream of resurrection, today we must lower our heads. This is our wish.'[46]

Citizens of Japan sit before their radios and hear their emperor's voice with lowered heads. Tears fall silently. Many perform hara-kiri and prepare for their next birth. Couples hand each other a sword to take their own lives. They can never live in a Japan that has surrendered.

A few days later

Everything is over. The Japanese have lost. Our struggle has halted. We haven't admitted defeat; we will continue to fight even if the British kill us like flies. We remain firm in our objectives and decisions. This is an order from our dear Netaji.

Today, I am remembering Ma. How must she be? Alone, her body riddled with arthritis. I cannot imagine what she must be feeling. I wonder how Tulu is taking care of her.

Who invented such a bomb? Every creature in contact with its winds of destruction becomes incapacitated—even healthy, strong soldiers. The bomb has spared nothing—the beauty of nature, the peace of the village, the gardens of the city—humans have destroyed even this. Only God can save us from the games this massacring bomb plays.

Thursday, 23 August 1945

In the morning, Ved enters and says: 'Netaji has died.'

'Dhat!' I say crossly.

'You don't believe me?'

'As if that could happen.'

He thinks for a while before agreeing. 'Accha, then I will think the same.'

What a strange person he is! If I don't believe something, does it mean he should also stop believing it? Anyway, people can think whatever they want.

The rest of us chat for a bit about incidental matters, and then we leave.

By the evening, news of Netaji's death has spread everywhere. So many rumours continue to fly that perhaps it's another gust of wind?

Panditji comes home in the evening and says: 'There was an accident at Taihoku Airport. It was a Japanese plane. Netaji got burnt badly. And Colonel Habib, too. Netaji passed away in Taihoku. Colonel Habib has taken his ashes to Japan.'

I hear all this. However, I feel an urge to laugh; how do men immediately believe whatever they hear? I don't believe this at all.

As I am writing, Mataji sits close by. She is crying, taking the name of Netaji. I say to her: 'What is there to cry about? We still don't know if this is the truth.'

Mataji responds: 'What do you know of the world yet, beti? How would you know what is death? And that too our Netaji—'

She begins crying again. That death causes grief is something even I know. But, in my understanding, death is unseen. For us, there should be no difference between living and dying. Is it possible that Netaji would leave us like this? No, these are all lies.

I say to her: 'Mataji, these rumours are definitely the work of a devil. Netaji cannot leave us and go. This is nothing but false propaganda.'

Friday, 24 August 1945

Even though the news of Netaji's death is false, we must mourn according to worldly customs. A group of Indians gather to remember him.

Panditji says: 'Our beloved Netaji left Bangkok on 23 July for Malaya and some other locations. He promised to meet me again. How can I say what happened to him or how it happened or what he experienced? On 14 August, Netaji broadcast from Shonan: "Comrades, all sorts of wild rumours are now afloat in Shonan and other places, one of them being that hostilities have ceased. Most of these rumours are either false or highly exaggerated. Do not yourselves be influenced in any manner by wild bazaar rumours. We have to face any situation that may arise, like brave soldiers fighting for the freedom of their Motherland." And, on 15 August, he said: "For the freedom of our country, we have faced and will continue to face many obstacles. Our fight does not end because Japan has raised a white flag or because the atom bombs have fallen. There are many paths to Delhi and we must never forget our duty. We must fulfil our duty as patriots with perseverance."'[47]

Panditji continues: 'On 18 August, he departed in an airplane with Habib Sahib and some Japanese officers.[48] The plane arrived in Taihoku, the capital of Formosa, in the afternoon and Netaji had lunch at 2 p.m. Everyone boarded the plane at 2.30 p.m. As soon as the airplane took off, its propeller fell off and the plane fell headlong into a cloud of flames. Netaji and his companions quickly tried to get off the plane, but Netaji was on fire. Even his head was on fire.'

As Panditji speaks, my heart deflates. Mataji starts crying, mumbling 'Netaji, Netaji'. Panditji gently squints at her and she becomes quiet. But I find everything unbelievable. I keep my hope up that Netaji will reappear before us. Panditji said that we must walk on the path set by Netaji. Our country will be free and before long. And that's why we will continue to march on. Netaji lives forever. Jai Hind.

We observe two minutes of silence in remembrance of Netaji. Ever since I met him, I became devoted to both the country and Netaji. This was not the so-called 'idolization' that some may think. It was the effect of his personality and leadership, which had left me electrified.

At the condolence meeting, I cannot express my grief. I have to complete the ritual, and so I do, but I am sure someday Netaji will rise before us again.

Saturday, 25 August 1945

A horde of American soldiers and officers barge into our house today. I was learning how to roll a roti with Mataji.

They threaten us with their bayonets and say: 'Come on, where are your documents? Papers?'

I laugh and say, 'What?'

'Documents, papers!'

'I will not tell you.' I am enjoying myself. I laugh at the meaningless display of their bayonets. We are only women and children in the house, and that too without weapons.

Mataji holds my arm. 'Beti, be quiet. Say nothing; these people can be very vicious.'

'What will they do?' I respond, walking straight up to my room. Raju and Swadesh Kumari follow me. The goras follow, too, carrying their bayonets.

Under Panditji's bed is a small trunk of mine. It is made of iron and has no key inserted. One gora kicks the box out from under the bed with his boot. He takes out the contents and tosses them around. He finds a revolver, given to me by Papa, nestled between sarees and frocks. He takes the revolver to his lieutenant and hangs the sarees from his shoulders. Papa's typewriter is also there, and he keeps it aside.

Sheela Bhabhi starts crying in fear. She presses a baby to her bosom and flees downstairs to Mataji. What the ill-mannered soldiers said to her I don't know. My eyes turn red with fury; my fists clasp shut. I mutter something in Japanese.

Looking at me, the American lieutenant says: 'Don't be so furious, young lady. You are defeated.' He says some other things, but I don't understand English well enough. I am incandescent; just looking at their faces is enough to infuriate me.

I look at him and say furiously: 'I shoot you.'

He laughs and tosses the revolver towards me. There are no bullets in it. It is pointless to take the revolver. If I succeed, I know they will pounce on me. Suddenly, an image of Ma appears before me. It feels as though she is in the room in front of me, her powerful gaze eyes me sternly. I can hear her voice: *Immediately give him the revolver.* I throw the revolver at the white demon.

I will never fear these white demons, but I do fear Ma. I am scared of her large, stern eyes, always clouded by some kind of sadness. I cannot keep any secrets from her. I cannot lie, even being so far away. The Yankees take valuables from Bhabhi's room, too, and leave. A strange silence—like the one after a storm—falls on the house. It feels as though a dramatic play has ended. I'm very regretful that my pistol and sarees will come of use to these Yankees.

Monday, 27 August 1945

Panditji does not return home from office. We hear that the British have captured him directly at his office. It was inevitable. We sit together with Mataji. She is a brave wife; she doesn't cry, but smiles and says: 'It is God's work. Whatever he wants will happen.'

The children eat and sleep. Anand Swarup and I sit with Mataji for dinner.

'If you don't eat, I won't eat either,' says Anand Swarup.

Mataji says: 'I'll eat; of course, I'll eat. What sadness do I have that I won't eat?'

We eat and go upstairs.

New daily routine

6 a.m. Wake up, have a bath
7–8 a.m. Studies
8 a.m. Breakfast; help Mataji get the children ready for school
12 p.m. Lunch; playtime with the children
2–3 p.m. Practise typing
4 p.m. A bath followed by playtime with the children
6 p.m. Dinner
7 p.m. Read a book and sleep

I have spent a month with Panditji's family. I have written my daily routine above and the days are passing on and on in the same manner. Sometimes I remember Papa or Ma, and I leave everything and lie down. On one such occasion, I see Ma coming to me, wearing a white saree, with a smile on her face. I am confused. I know I have not yet fallen asleep. She comes up to me, but as soon as I get up and say 'Ma' she vanishes. I flounder in my thoughts—helpless but hopeful. She was looking exquisite.

When I tell Anand Swarup this, he says it must be telepathy. 'Whatever you think, you'll be able to see.'

I say: 'Ma must also be thinking about me.'

***

Ever since Panditji has been imprisoned, Mataji has been looking lifeless. They are both brave wives—Ma and Mataji—but there is such a difference between both of them. One is a stone; the other, a flower. They both walk on the path taken by their respective husbands, becoming their shadows. They have never expressed their difficulties to their husbands.

I have heard that the enemies have been searching for Papa for many days. They are trying to trap him. But Papa will never admit defeat. Seeing Ma in person today makes me very sad. Who knows when I will meet her again? Will there ever be a miraculous evening when we all gather under the same roof?

***

The world has been divided into two groups—the victors and the losers. Both groups are swimming in the same seas of terror. The victors cannot make sense of their victory—the excessive expense of human lives has led to an economic disaster. What is there to say about the desperation of the losers? People say that there is nothing known as morality left in Japan.

In Bangkok, the American forces are robbing everything possible. They've imprisoned all Indian patriots, and they go into the homes of Indian businessmen and loot whatever possible. In Thailand, there has also been some fighting between some rebellious locals and the police. The rebels dress as robbers and live in the jungles. They sometimes attack the police quarters. These rebels are against the Thai king and are fighting to end dynastic rule. The same group killed King Bhumibol's elder brother, King Ananda. Last night, we could hear bullets being fired continuously.

Several days later

Today, I go with Mataji to meet Panditji. I am in a large hall with a stage and see ten–twelve gentlemen biding their time. Behind the stage, there are arrangements for a toilet.

One Sindhi brother says: 'Oof, at least they should have given us a blade to shave our beards.'

Panditji is sitting with them. Seeing me, he laughs in his usual manner and says: 'Arre, come, come.'

Mataji has brought some items to eat. They all quickly open the boxes and eat makki ki roti, sarson ka saag and aloo-paneer sabzi. The Indians from Gorakhpur are supplying the prisoners with plenty of milk and curd. (Many people from Gorakhpur and Chhapra have settled in Southeast Asia. They are usually involved in the milk business.)

A few minutes later, a British officer enters and asks us to leave. We speak to Panditji briefly and then exit the hall.

A few days later

The British have sent our patriots, including Panditji, to Singapore. The brightness of our heroes will never be dimmed.

Before departing, Ved Prakash comes to meet us one last time. He says: 'We will meet on the other side of the Hooghly river.'

Today, like all days, I help Mataji with the prayer rituals. We sing a combination of kirtans and nationalistic songs. The music lifts up our spirits.

Part Three

March–April 1946[49]

The days are passing by us quickly. I keep myself busy doing housework; I have learnt how to polish brass and bronze vessels, and enjoy the process thoroughly. The more I polish, the more the vessels gleam. I also enjoy reading the Mahabharata and the Ramayana. I ask Mataji to explain the parts I do not understand. Each and every tale has a sermon or message in it.

The Indian patriots imprisoned by the British in Singapore are returning home today. They were released last week, but did not receive permission to leave the island city. The British government knows the situation is precarious—the people of India are angry. They can do anything. The armed forces may also rebel at any moment. The British cannot afford to sentence our heroes nor can they leave them in jail for long. They know they need to tread delicately, and so they have hastily released many prisoners.

I knot two garlands, expecting Papa to return with Panditji. Mataji has prepared Panditji's favourite vegetables—aloo-mattar-paneer sabzi—to be served with makki ki roti. Ma did the same whenever Papa returned from distant lands. She cleaned the house, spruced up us children, and even took time to beautify her appearance. She would wear an apron, and then make roti, moong dal, and Papa's favourite vegetables and meat dishes. I have gotten into the habit of comparing Mataji and Ma in their behaviour and their temperament. Today, I notice as sprightly and jovial as Ma is, Mataji is patient and gentle in equal measure. One expresses her feelings in happiness, the other says everything is work and quietly makes makki ki roti.

I am that jovial, spirited mother's daughter. I enter Panditji's room, and quickly clean the sofa and dust the decorative items. Anand Swarup, Mahaveer and Swaraj Kumari help me.

Panditji returns at dusk. The car stops in front of the house and people start chanting slogans to welcome him. A delightful moment quickly transforms into a moment of despair for me. Panditji steps out of the vehicle. But not Papa. The car leaves. Is he still in Singapore? Swinging between a death sentence and freedom? As Panditji comes up the stairs, I place two garlands around his neck and say: 'Jai Hind.'

His face hasn't changed—the same brightness and that same unfettered laugh. A blue sky lit by golden rays. Looking at him, I remember Raja Dasharatha. Everyone is quiet and emotional. Mataji is standing behind me, wiping her tears. We come to the courtyard, and Panditji sits on a cot.

I say to him, 'Please remove your shoes; you can wash up and eat your dinner.' It feels as though I am his eldest daughter, forgetting that I have no relationship with him or his family. I have never received this much love and affection from anywhere else. Where else would I feel so at ease? At home?

Guests begin arriving, and Panditji goes and sits on the sofa without washing or eating.

He comes back after an hour and relishes the makki ki roti and vegetables that are served.

Monday, 22 April 1946

In the evening, Panditji returns home with a letter in his hand and flies up the stairs. Even though I am curious about the letter,

I deflect my interest by asking another question: 'Pitaji, whose photo is that in the shrine?'

Panditji lowers his voice and says: 'Do not ask Mataji this question; she will start crying. That is our eldest son, Vasudev. He lives in America and is training to be a motor engineer.'

Oh, I had already asked Mataji and tears had dripped from her cheeks. Trying to change the subject again, I blurt: 'What's in the envelope?' It looks like an official government envelope, which makes me apprehensive. In this world, good news is rare while bad news overflows.

I notice a smile on Panditji's lips. Inside the envelope is a letter from Papa—the British have released him. He had been sentenced to hang and was soon to be banished to Kala Pani, the Cellular Jail in the Andaman Islands. But thanks to the intervention of Pandit Nehru and several Congress ministers, he has been released.

Burma, Singapore and Malaya are overflowing with soldiers and officers of the British Army. They have heard tales of the INA and its bravery, as well as Netaji's miracles. While the British are calling soldiers of the INA traitors and persecuting them, the All India Congress Committee is defending them. They state: 'Giving a punishment to the people who worked for India's independence—the Indian National Army—is inappropriate and its result will not be good.' They have established the INA Defence Committee and have taken the cases of members of the INA into their own hands.

Papa is staying with Captain Mitra in Singapore. He asks me to join him quickly. Hearing the news, Mataji first laughs with joy and then quickly slips into the depths of sorrow. She says: 'Asha rani is my daughter. Where will she go? Why don't we call Sahayji here instead?'

Panditji and Mataji ask me to leave for Singapore in two weeks. But I cannot remain here for a single day more. Panditji senses my restless mind.

It is nine at night, and I am feeling remorseful. I should have immediately agreed to Mataji's suggestion. I need to keep in mind other people's feelings, too. Tomorrow, as soon as I get up, I will tell Mataji to ask Papa to come to Bangkok. We will stay here together.

Wednesday, 8 May 1946

Perhaps this is what you call a metamorphosis—from a clumsy teenager to a soldier willing to be beheaded for the country. From a student of Showa Kojo College to a Vaishnava girl drowning in the tales of the Mahabharata and the Ramayana, a sister—a pehenji—busy with housework and childcare. I am standing at a crossroads—able to look back and laugh at myself. I will be separated from a doting set of parents today to return to my father.

I have to reach the airport at seven in the morning. I rise at 5 a.m. and get ready. Mataji comes into the room with pooris and sooji ka halwa. I have been drenched with love and affection over the past year. I feel an urge to wrap myself around Mataji, a symbol of unrestrained love. But my body does not listen to the commands of my mind. I stand still, frozen like a statue, staring at Mataji. She places the food down and puts two voile sarees into my suitcase. Panditji had also given me a beautiful silk saree last evening.

I wear the voile saree given by Mataji. I cannot eat, but sit through the ceremony of breakfast. All the children come to see me. Rajo wraps herself tightly around me; it feels like she will never let go. I lift her to my hips and proceed down the stairs.

Mataji succumbs to her emotions—tears flood past the dam of her eyes and flow freely down her cheeks.

I continue to stand firm, composed. Let the tears fall, I think angrily to myself. Suddenly, I feel myself bending and touching Mataji's feet. Netaji had said: 'Touching feet is a symbol of subordination—those who lower their heads do not go to have their heads cut off.' I still agree with his words, but the moment propels my head to lower itself. My fingers touch her feet, and I feel blessed. When I was bidding farewell to Ma, my brother and sisters in Tokyo, the situation demanded a rocklike heart and a firm countenance. In today's farewell, I am surrounded by affectionate people who encircle me like the tender rays of the dawn sun.

I reach the airport on time. I say 'Jai Hind' to everyone in the lounge and proceed with Panditji to the plane. Below the steps, I stand at attention and say 'Jai Hind' to Panditji.

'Do not forget us,' he says.

I respond, 'Phir milenge, na?'

We burst out laughing. We will meet again.

From the lounge window, I can see the children and hear them beckoning me. 'Pehenji, Pehenji!' I wave and enter the plane. I know no home, no one place that is mine—the war has unravelled everything. How then can I have a fixed place to sit on the plane? I am standing idly when two young British men stand up and offer their seats. Gestures are the trademark of the British—a tool they use to enslave both people and countries. Looking at these goras, it is inevitable that I will become angry.

'No,' I respond, and continue to stand indifferently.

A Sindhi gentleman comes up to me and says: 'Behenji, please sit here.'

'Meherbani.' I thank him with a smile, and sit down, glowering at the British men as I pass by them. They stare back as though I am an uncultured element. My behaviour later becomes a source of tickling satisfaction. I have insulted the enemies of my country, the people who are responsible for the martyrdom of thousands, and for the death of Netaji. Even though I know this act won't achieve anything, it helps clear the damp fog in my mind.

Behind me, my Indian brother also finds a seat. We chat for a bit and then begin analysing the character of our enemy. About three hours later, I feel the plane descend and I remove the cotton buds that are stuffed in my ears. The plane lowers itself over Singapore's airport. It slides down the runway and stops directly in front of the airport building.

The Indian brothers take me towards the building. Papa is standing in the hall. Spontaneously I join my hands together and say, 'Jai Hind.' I notice he has become very thin.

'Arre, you've become exactly like an Indian girl,' he says in surprise.

I introduce the Indian brother who accompanies me. 'This brother has come with me—' Then I realize I don't know his name. By then, he also leaves, and I don't have to go through the formality of asking his name.

A taxi takes us to Dr Mitra's house. Mrs Mitra—or Mashima as I call her—reminds me of Ma. She is buzzing like a bee, busy with her work, keeping the children in strict discipline, briefly showering them with affection. Their daughter, Lakshmi, becomes a friend very quickly. Her younger brothers stare at me with sparkling eyes, desiring to speak, but drowning in shyness.

Papa presents me with a beautiful saree from Varanasi.

Papa and I chat till late that night. Then I go to my room (actually Lakshmi's room) and write a letter to Ma. And then my nightcap—this diary!

Today, I have regained Papa. Let's see when I will be reunited with Ma as well.

May 1946

Papa and I chat late into the night. We share stories of our months apart. Here are some of Papa's tales in his own words...

I went to Saigon without telling you. People thought Netaji had sent me to collect donations and to open a branch of the Indian Independence League. The truth was something else—something extremely important and secretive. My true motive was to go from Saigon to Hanoi. Over there, I was to have talks with members of the Chinese Communist Party and make arrangements to go to Manchuria. Since the Russians and British had separated, we believed we could join hands with the Russians in Manchuria and use their help to win our freedom.

However, the war ended sooner than we anticipated. I was in Hanoi and desperately wanted to meet Netaji in Saigon. But I did not get a plane from the Japanese. Hence, I had to continue staying in Hanoi along with Colonel Chatterji, Major Hasan, Shri Debnath Das, Colonel Gulzara Singh and Colonel Pritam Singh.

We all stayed in Hanoi till end-December 1945. I met General Ho Chi Minh and we became close friends. The Chinese forces took north Vietnam into their possession and the Anglo-American forces took the south. When the Chinese forces came to Hanoi, I met their commander, General Lu Han.[50] I told him that my companions and I wish to be imprisoned. I requested him to arrest us.

General Lu Han said: 'Why, are you the enemies of China? Who is your enemy?'

I responded: 'Our enemy is only one, and that is the British government. We are not enemies of China.'

To that he said: 'Oh, then your enemy and our enemy is one. You are our enemy's enemy. Then you are our friends and I cannot imprison you. You can stay within Hanoi city with freedom.'

He promised to keep us safe. My companions and I stayed in Hanoi without difficulties. On 21 December 1945, General Lu Han took time out to meet us and tell us the British were about to imprison us. Colonel Wilson, who was with the British mission, had come to know that my companions and I were in Hanoi, and had made enquiries about us.

The following day, when Colonel Wilson appeared, I said: 'I had come to know yesterday that you were going to arrest me. If I wanted to, I could have run away. By doing this, I would have proved myself to be a coward, which I didn't want. I have already made arrangements and am ready for you. I can withstand all sorts of difficulties.'

I then handed myself over to Colonel Wilson.

From Hanoi, we were brought to Singapore. Colonel Chatterji, Major Hasan, Shri Thivy and I were kept in Pearl Hill Prison.[51] Colonel Gulzara Singh and Colonel Pritham Singh were kept in Changi Prison. We stayed in Pearl Hill Prison till 30 March 1946. From 1 April, civil administration restarted in Singapore. They did not want to keep the prisoners of the Indian National Army. We were too many in number, and, within the country and outside, everyone supported us. We were never scared. Whenever we were asked anything, we would respond in clear, articulate words.

For their thousand questions of 'Why?' we had one answer: 'For freedom.'

On 1 April 1946, I exited the gates of the jail wearing my complete INA uniform. All my companions and the jail officials looked in my direction in surprise.

I learnt from Sharmaji that Netaji had handed you over to him and then left. I wanted to meet Netaji, but wasn't able to. Anyway, I am walking on the path set by him. I asked the British officers to send you to Singapore safely.

A few days later

I am strolling in Dr Mitra's garden when I notice a few Japanese prisoners cleaning drains under the supervision of some American soldiers. I feel an urge to talk to my Japanese brothers. Feeling sympathetic, I take a cigarette from Papa's packet with a matchstick, and walk towards them.

'Ohayo gozaimasu,' I greet them.

Their faces flood with light. I give them the cigarette. They lower their heads several times and say, 'Arigato.'

They light the cigarette.

An American officer is observing us. He comes up to me and asks with a smile: 'May I have a cigarette, please?'

In reply, he receives an acrid look from me. When I return indoors, I tell Papa about what had transpired. He laughs slowly, deeply.

'Why are you laughing?' I ask.

'You should have given him the cigarette.'

'Why should I? They're our enemies. They are the ones who dropped an atom bomb on Japan. They destroyed Japan. And I should give them a cigarette?'

Papa reflects on my words, and says: 'No comment.'

End-May 1946

It's been twenty days since I arrived in Singapore. What a small but important island this is—a land desired by many nations. The east and west stand here, eyeball to eyeball, destroying each other. Once it was Singapore, then it became Shonan, and now it is Singapore again.

We have been requested to visit many Indian families. Officers of the British Army keep coming to meet Papa. They want to hear about the INA and the Azad Hind Government in his own words. After all, they too are Indians—the fires of patriotism must be sparking within them, especially after hearing the brave tales of their brothers and Netaji.

Papa and I have been to meet Commissioner Sahib several times, hoping he will give us permission to return to India.[52] But he remains a representative of the British government. How can he disobey the commands of *his* government? We, the lovers of Netaji, obey the commands of the Azad Hind Government. Netaji said it was inevitable that we will need to observe the directions of the Indian government after independence. However, as long as the Union Jack flutters over India's head, we will rapturously obey Netaji's instructions and will work towards expelling the British from our country.

This is why Papa is speaking to these officials in a saccharine tone. But Papa never lowers his head. Those who are willing to get beheaded do not lower their heads. In jail, the British spent hours questioning Papa, hoping he would reveal something in a moment of desperation. Papa responded to all questions clearly, fearlessly—we have done no thievery; we have fought for our country. Now everyone is restless for India's independence. All of India has risen together, inspired by the stories of our bravery. The days of the 1857 Revolt and Jallianwala Bagh are gone. The days of atrocities are over. The British have to tread with caution. They cannot stop our freedom.

***

I write Ma a letter. I've written to her several times, but I never receive a reply. How can I get one? It seems all ships belonging to Japan are sinking one by one. And who knows how reliable the boats are? Clever British detectives have spread their webs all over East Asia. They suspect everyone and everything—even a letter between a mother and daughter—fearing some hidden meaning behind the words. As if we, the lovers of India, will hide anything? As if we can hide our love for India? Hearing India's name or Netaji's name brings tears to our eyes. Singing '*Shubh sukh chain*' or '*Jana gana mana*' makes our eyes moist. Then what question is there of hiding anything? Anyway, detectives have to be emotionless. There is nothing in them other than lies, betrayal and conspiracy.

Some weeks later

I am working in the kitchen with Lakshmi when the door suddenly opens and a man with a long, unkempt beard appears. We both cautiously step back.

'Who is it?' I demand loudly.

I can see the crook of a smile appear on the stranger's face. He stands uncomfortably close and says: 'Arre, it's me, Asha. Zara jaldi se ek cup chai banakar do.'

It is Satya Kaka's voice and his catchphrase: 'Make me a cup of tea.' Recognizing him, I become joyous.

'Kaka, what kind of face—' I say, then halt my words to make a cup of tea and shove it into his hands. He pours the tea onto the saucer and begins drinking it. In the meantime, I place some tea, sugar and powdered milk in a packet and tie it shut. He drinks the tea, picks up the packet, and vanishes. What his next destination is … I can only wonder.

Satyadev Sahay—or Satya Kaka—is the director of the Intelligence Bureau of the Azad Hind Government, responsible for the well-being of Netaji. The British, ruffled by his past activities, are investigating him and keenly seeking his whereabouts. I learn the story of how they eventually catch him much later, from Kaka himself. These are his words:

> In Singapore, I lived in front of Netaji's house. When there was an issue with the Indian diaspora in Seremban (Malaya), Netaji decided to visit and I accompanied him. We were in Seremban when we learnt about the atom bombs and the subsequent Japanese surrender. Along with Ayer Sahib, we returned to Singapore from Seremban. Further plans were made in Singapore.
>
> It was here that Netaji gave me the order to go underground. It was extremely important for me to do this. The British wouldn't have benefited much from capturing a minister or an officer as they would have from capturing a secret service fellow. If they caught me, they would have definitely lynched me and left me half-dead. Perhaps they wouldn't have even stopped there. They would've been unsuccessful in getting anything out of me and would have handed me a terrible death in frustration.
>
> Netaji did not like this thought. Hence, the very next day, I retreated into Malaya's jungles. I used to return occasionally and gather news. I once sent you a telegram in Shanti's name from Port Dickson. Perhaps you got it. Bhaiya was in Pearl Hill barracks at this time. One day I

learnt that Pandit Nehru had arrived in Singapore. He was staying in Adelphi Hotel.[53] I needed to speak to him about some important matters. I returned to the city and saw the hotel was surrounded by armed guards. It was not possible for me to meet him.

I made another attempt to see Nehruji later that night. I sent a message to him via a trusted man. At around midnight, I jumped over the back wall of the hotel and entered the hotel periphery. Using a drainpipe for support, I clambered up the wall and, with much difficulty, reached Pandit Nehru's room. As soon as I spotted his room, the door opened. It was Nehruji waiting for me. Upon seeing me, he hugged me and said: 'My son, bravo!' We spoke about some other important matters.

He then said: 'Now you can surrender yourself to the British. They can no longer touch another member of the Azad Hind Government.' After a while, I exited his room and left the hotel the same way, jumping over the back wall. I stopped to wait for a bus. I had just reached the bus stop when American soldiers surrounded me. Before I realized what had happened, there were handcuffs on my wrists.

They kept me imprisoned for two months. The British assaulted me with sharp questions, and though I did not give the answer to even a single question, they never tortured me. This is due to Nehruji's influence and help. Today, after two months, I have been released and have come here.

Kaka never speaks about his difficulties, but I can estimate the problems he faced in the jungles myself.

Anyway, let's see when we get to return to India.

June 1946

Today Dr Pal Chowdhury arrived. Papa and I go with him to see the coast. When Singapore was Shonan, the Japanese created a war memorial in remembrance of the patriots who had lost their lives. And then when Shonan became Singapore again, American officers ordered Japanese prisoners of war to tear down the memorial. In the same location, they have constructed an American memorial pillar. I see Japanese prisoners planting flowers around the pillar, even placing bouquets at the location.

I ask them: 'Why are you putting flowers and such things?'

'Death makes everybody one,' responds one prisoner. 'Wherever the souls of our brave Japanese martyrs go, the souls of the American martyrs go, too. Friends and enemies exist here—not in the other realm. They have fulfilled their duty for their country—as have we. It is natural to pay tribute to all patriots.'

He then smiles.

I remember the Japanese phrase 'bushi no nasake', which means the compassion of the warrior. Pity, compassion and the ability to forgive are specialities of Japanese warriors.

Saturday, 22 June 1946

We have received permission from the British commissioner to depart for India. I rise at 4 a.m. and get ready. We then bid Dr Mitra, Mashima, Lakshmi and everyone else farewell. These people, too, have become ours. I do not feel sadness while saying goodbye. How many have I met and slipped away from? It has become a part of my daily routine. To say that we'll meet again has become an empty courtesy because the wish to reunite seems impossible to realize.

The rapture of going to India has made me forget Singapore entirely. We smile and say, 'Jai Hind.' Mashima is wiping her tears, but I do not go near her, rigid as I am. Still, while standing near the steps of the plane, I quickly blurt out, 'Mashima, we will meet again in Calcutta,' and speedily go inside.

Tearing past a sky scented with dawn, the plane flies westwards.

***

I see the Bay of Bengal for the first time. When we reach the border between Thailand and Burma, I first see dense jungles, and then, in the south, the thoughtful, lapping waves of the bay. It is like looking into the fluttering pages of history—as though each wave carries with it a story of a historical marvel or disaster. How many ferries, boats and ships must have sunk in this bay? How many lovers of India, how many invaders must be spending sleepless nights under this sea? War and peace are two states. Both are symbols of power—with the only difference being that one is a destructive force and the other a creative force. These two forces can never meet as one. They both chase each other in circles.

A little while later, we land in an airport in Burma. We take a terrible road from the airport to Rangoon and reach Bashir Kaka's house (S.M. Bashir, a member of the IIL). Papa and Bashir Kaka speak for several hours. They both get lost in wartime memories. It is here in Rangoon, under the shadow of Netaji, that they fought rapturously. The atom bomb has destroyed everything. They had comprehensive plans of marching to India, but the massacre in Japan has undone everything.

Anyway, our struggle is not yet over—it is just beginning. In the evening, we meet friends of Papa's. And later that night, at close to 10 p.m., Papa, Bashir Kaka and I go secretively into the jungles. A friend of Papa's is hiding here—Thakin Aung San. San is the leader of the Revolutionary Party and the prime minister of Burma. The two of them had made grand plans ... But everything is now finished. New plans will be made again. I also speak to his daughter Suu Kyi.

Our struggle for independence is not yet complete. This peace is not true; it is temporary, the eye of a storm. The days are fast coming when this Bay of Bengal and all the nations traversing it will come under the watch of Free India.

Sunday, 23 June 1946

Departure from Rangoon. Tearing through the blue skies, our plane advances towards India. We cross Burma's thick jungles, with rivers snaking through them, and reach the Bay of Bengal once again. Its shimmering waves ebb along the coastline, before thrusting into the dark shadows of the beautiful forests.

Satya Kaka blossoms with joy and exuberance. 'Asha, once we reach, you must salute everyone and say Jai Hind.'

'Ji,' I agree, thinking but not saying aloud: I already know this.

I notice Papa's eyes are moist; he is emotional, tears as salty as the waters beneath us. I have always seen Papa laughing, but today, he releases a barrage of emotions through his tears. After twenty-five long years, he is to be reunited with his motherland. Without his mother. Without my mother.

His mother—my grandmother—had toiled through the years, awaiting the return of her two sons. And then, unable to wait any longer, she joined the divine spirit. Today, Papa is returning to his country, incomplete. What his mental state must have been at this moment, after all that he had experienced and suffered, only he can share.

Our plane descends over Calcutta's Dum Dum Airport. A large crowd gathers, which includes some members of the Azad Hind Relief Committee. Everyone embraces Papa and Kaka.

As instructed, I say 'Jai Hind' to everyone. Suddenly someone comes up to me and pulls my nose with the words: 'Eh, Asha. How tall you have become!'

Who is this person who has the courage to pull my nose?

I am staring at him in amazement when Papa comes up to me and says: 'Arre, this is your uncle.'

I look at the man again. And then Bengali explodes from my mouth: 'Apni amaar mama.'

Everyone begins laughing. I had never imagined that someone would pull my nose the instant I reached India. There is one more person who is not wearing a dhoti–kurta, but a khaki-coloured military-style suit. I salute and, in response, he accepts my salute. He introduces himself as L.P. Choudhry, a friend of Kaka's. He is the secretary of the Calcutta Welcome Committee. He is quite overbearing.

Our car traverses through the streets of Calcutta. What roads they are! In the middle, cows and calves sit placidly, and no one makes the slightest effort to remove them. Instead, vehicles weave past them. I know we pray to cows in our country, but I can't imagine any objection to removing them. The scene looks bizarre.

We go straight to Hindustan Park, to the house of my grandmother, Urmila Devi, sister of Chittaranjan Das. We go up the stairs and are greeted by Didima's dominating figure looming large in the middle of the hall.

Papa and Kaka touch her feet and say 'pranaam', while indicating that I should do the same. I am wearing my cap, so I first salute with a loud 'Jai Hind' before removing it. I then bend forward and touch her two small feet. Gigantic Didima's hands and feet are tiny in comparison to her body.

She speaks in Bengali: 'Hoye che do.' That's enough; now go wear a saree. My two aunts, wives of Ma's brothers, take me inside. We all begin chatting in Bengali. I freshen up and change into a saree.

There is a rally at four in the evening in Deshapriya Park. After Papa's speech, I sing '*Shubh sukh chain*'.

We stay in Calcutta for three days. We visit Netaji's house and meet his relatives, and also visit the INA relief camp. On the fourth day, we depart for Delhi.

Wednesday, 26 June 1946

From Calcutta, we go straight to Delhi, and stay at the residence of Mrs Aruna Asaf Ali. We meet many patriots who are leading India's independence movement, including Mahatma Gandhi (Bapu), Dr Rajendra Prasad and Jawaharlal Nehru.

I touch Bapu's feet and, in return, I receive a slap on my back as blessings. Rajendra Babu turns to Bapu and says: 'This is Sati's daughter. Twenty years ago, Anand Mohan took Sati and ran away to Japan; he has just returned.'

Rajendra Babu smiles softly and begins chatting with Papa in Bhojpuri.

Bapu asks me: 'Asha, are you Bengali or Bihari?'

'I am Hindustani,' I say, the words involuntarily spilling out of my mouth.

Bapu laughs and says: 'This girl is very clever. Rajendra Babu and Sarat Babu are both here. If she said she was Bihari, Sarat Babu would get upset.' Sarat Chandra Bose is Netaji's elder brother. He continues: 'And if she said she was Bengali, Rajendra Babu would get angry. That's why she's saying Hindustani...'

I quickly disagree. 'No, Bapu. I am Hindustani.'

Papa comes closer and says: 'Bapu, my children know nothing of caste and regionalism, and so on.'

Nehruji then inspects me and says: 'There is still a lot to be done. Learn Hindi; then only will you be able to do something for the nation.'

His daughter, Indiraji, points at a Chinese flower vase in the living room and asks the meaning of the symbol drawn on it. I explain that the Chinese character 'chaju' is written on the vase, meaning long life or immortality.

***

Sarojini Naidu calls us over that evening; she has organized a dinner party. I dress in a saree and attempt to look presentable. Papa, to the best of his ability, pulls my hair into a bun. Looking at my saree and bun, Naiduji gets upset. In a throaty, koel-like voice, she says: 'Oh! Asha, go back and wear your Rani of Jhansi Regiment uniform. Sahayji, please take her back.'

We return home. I quickly slip into my full uniform, including britches and coat, and happily return to the party. This time, Naiduji praises and appreciates me with an open heart.

Embarrassed, I say: 'Please talk about Papa and Kaka, not about me. What have I even done yet?'

'Why?' she responds. 'If I don't say it, then how will these girls dressed in georgette sarees ever learn the meaning of sacrifice?'

A few weeks later

From Delhi we go to Lahore. Then via Karachi, Hyderabad (Sindh Province), Bombay and Varanasi, we reach Patna. I have never studied India's geography, but learn a lot through my own eyes. In every city, crowds welcome us with loud celebrations. At all gatherings Papa gives a speech, and at the end, I sing '*Shubh sukh chain*'.

But I always feel a strange jolt. What have I done for the country yet? Papa and Kaka's service to the nation is worth the loudest praises. But my service to the nation has just begun. When I share my difficulties with Papa and Kaka, they say: 'Do not worry pointlessly. Strength is on your side. March ahead in high spirits.'

A few months later

I meet my uncles after twelve long years at Patna station. Together we go to a gathering at the Patna Lawns (later renamed as Gandhi Maidan). After Papa's stormy speech, Colonel Mehboob and some others come to me and ask me to say a few words. They leave me with no choice.

I gather my courage and stand in front of the microphone, and say: 'Brothers and sisters…' And then, in one long breath: 'I am a soldier. I know how to fight for freedom. I may not know how to speak, but I know how to fight and die for the country. Please push your bodies and minds to the limit for our freedom. Jai Hind!'

I quickly sit back down. I can hear the gurgling sound of clapping. The vast crowd is smiling and jumping jubilantly in front of me. I am covered in sweat. I understand why Kaka does not come to these gatherings. He and I are both soldiers. We can never become politicians. A person like Papa is a skilled politician—the moment he speaks, he fills us with excitement, inspiration and courage.

Two days later

We spend two busy days in Patna and then one night in the house of my youngest aunt, Deviji Sahay, in Aarah. Deviji Bua's house is palatial, made in an old-world style. It is clean, and I realize that the most ordinary homes have delicious food.

I wake up at dawn and get ready. We all go to the station. Many people join us on the journey to Bhagalpur—both Congress men and women, as well as relatives. Debates transpire throughout the journey. At Bhagalpur station, we are again welcomed with slogans and chants. My uncles and the people of Nathnagar want us to reach our ancestral home in Purani Sarai as early as possible. But the people of Bhagalpur do not agree. They take us to the Muslim High School, where a public meeting has been organized. We are exhausted, but we have to give in to the excitement and happiness of the people of Bhagalpur.

But before we can proceed, we have to deal with the War of the Two Welcome Committees. Both committees are arguing vociferously about who will lead our procession to Nathnagar.

Papa says: 'I don't want any kind of fight or argument. I will reach home by myself.'

Then both committees conclude they will take the procession out together.

I whisper to Kaka: 'These people are fighting so much among themselves.'

'You'll see a lot more tamasha as the days pass,' he responds. 'We'll keep busy with our work.'

Our procession leaves from Sandis Compound. Papa, Kaka and I stand in a jeep, and salute everyone as we pass. People throng both sides of the road. Chants and slogans echo around us. We remain standing for the entire journey. This is not difficult for us—we are the warriors of Azad Hind.

When we reach Champanagar crossing, Papa and Kaka look excited and emotional.

Papa says: 'Nathnagar is exactly like we left it twenty-five years ago. There has been no change.'

All our relatives, along with the villagers and members of the procession gather around our house. Papa touches the threshold of the house, takes a pinch of earth from the ground and presses it against his forehead. I enjoy watching him.

We sit in a large hall called the darbar. I want to sit near Papa, but Chacha (Madan Mohan Sahay) indicates that I should follow him. It has become evening; it is dark inside the mud house. A lantern is burning in the corner. Madan Chacha takes me past a large courtyard into a room. The room is dark, with a flame flickering in the corner. It feels as though two people are standing and whispering over the flame.

Madan Chacha says: 'These are your aunts. Say pranaam.'

I say 'Jai Hind' and salute since I am in uniform. The aunts start laughing and also say, 'Jai Hind.' Their bright teeth are visible in the darkness.

Madan Chacha says: 'Touch their feet…'

The aunts protest. 'Nahi, nahi…'

***

After having a bath, we eat paratha with vegetables. Papa eats sattu (roasted gram flour) with milk, and a banana. I have been given a small room. I am sick and tired of the mosquitoes and the heat. Papa comes into the room, coughing. The aunts quickly cover their heads with their sarees, pinching the ends with their mouths. I laugh. A bubbling laughter. Papa, too, starts laughing with me. He spends some time with me on the cot, before rising. The men sit and sleep outside. Papa and Kaka will also sleep outside in the open fields.

The next day

I awake in the morning and step into the courtyard. On all four sides, there are small rooms. In one corner, there is a bathing house with a toilet attached. There is no roof over the bathing house. I bathe under the open skies with water drawn from a well. After bathing, I am helped into a saree. Papa and the other men go indoors for breakfast. The women stand and pull the ends of their sarees over their heads, and say pranaam to their elders.

I do the same and Papa says: 'Asha, what are you doing?'

I reply in Japanese: 'I'm doing the same as everyone else.'

We speak briefly in Japanese. We have chuda-dahi (flattened rice with curd) for breakfast. Then we go outside. After changing into my uniform, we go by car to TNB College for a meeting. From there, we go to the White House—the palace of Abhay Babu—where we have been invited for lunch. Abhay Babu's wife tries to make me wear bangles. But my hands are large and heavy. These hands and wrists are made for rifles, not delicate bangles.

Third day in Bhagalpur

In Purani Sarai, everything—every person, every second—seems strange to me. Sometimes I am speechless; sometimes I laugh.

I visit a village called Bhatoriya with Papa. All the zamindars of Purani Sarai have fields here; they grow several types of grains. We then travel to a distant village by elephant. The mahout positions a ladder to help us climb onto the elephant. I have just started to climb when Kaka's friend, Dr L.P. Choudhry from the welcome committee, approaches to help me.

'There's no need,' I protest. 'I can climb by myself.'

Twenty minutes later, we reach another village. I have a lot of fun travelling by elephant.

After we dismount, Satya Kaka says softly to me: 'If anyone comes to help you, you shouldn't refuse.'

'But, Kaka, why should someone hold my hand? I am a soldier. I don't need help.'

We reach home at six in the evening. I have a bath and wear a skirt with a top. My aunt, Chand Bua, objects: 'Wear a saree. You can't wear a skirt here…'

'But, Chand Bua,' I say, 'it's so hot here.'

'No, no. You must wear a saree. Men come and go. What will they say?'

Helpless, I change into a saree which Ma had gifted me several years ago. I have been taught to obey my elders from a young age. I have to listen to my aunt.

On the fifth day, we leave for Patna. Chand Bua and Phool Bua come with us, along with Chand Bua's daughter, Anu.

Papa's uncle, Rashbihari Lal, a member of the Legislative Assembly, gives us quarters to lodge in. This apartment has everything—tap water, electricity and much more.

I am scared of visiting Purani Sarai. The place does not make me feel good. But I know I must visit occasionally. It's Papa and Kaka's birthplace. They obviously like it.

I'm hoping Ma, Tulu, Baby and Ashok return to India quickly. But will they like it here?

Several months later

We are staying in R Block in Patna. Papa is forever busy on tours and Kaka is occupied making household arrangements. They will soon go to Japan on business, and to bring Ma and the others back. I have heard that Nehruji has made arrangements for Ma's medical care in Japan—army doctors have been sent to treat her rheumatic arthritis at home in Ogikubo. Nehruji has also made arrangements to bring them back to India.

My aunts and uncles stay with us, taking care of me, while Papa and Kaka are occupied with other matters. While there is a lot of activity, the lively atmosphere that Ma brings to the home is missing. My mind seems as hollow as this house. My aunts and uncles are teaching me a lot; I know I need to learn Indian customs, but all I can see is a lot of pretence and fabrication. For example, girls from good homes should not touch a broom. Or the fact that we eat khichdi (rice and lentils) at home, but call it pulao in front of others. If we spend ten rupees, we must say we have spent a hundred rupees. Why? Who is to benefit from this hypocrisy? We are all slaves. The British insult us and instruct us to salute the Union Jack. Eating khichdi is not an insult. As long as we are enslaved, the world will not respect us.

Anyway, I am young. I cannot say anything to the elders. Ma and Papa will reason with them. Yes, Chand Bua has changed quite a bit since our arrival. She is wearing hand-spun clothes and is taking military education. It is a beginning, and that is enough.

July 1947

Ma has returned. They left Tokyo on Baby's birthday—19 May—and boarded a ship that docked at a port in Madras in July.[54] Our reunion is awkward. Even before the war—before I received my military training—I struggled to display my emotions. And so, when I first see Ma, I smile a little, stand straight and say: 'Jai Hind.' Bua instructs me to place a garland around Ma's neck and to touch her feet. But Ma doesn't like this behaviour and nor do I; it is unnatural for us. Ma looks at me and becomes sad; I've become very thin and dark. But even she knows that her flowerlike daughter has become a soldier. I am the lioness who will fight in the jungle, under the sun, under the stormiest skies. This is who I need to be.

All day we are entangled in a knot of people. Once free, we chat late into the night. Then, when everyone has fallen asleep, Tulu and I begin whispering. Our conversations are special and remain between the two of us. It feels as though nothing has changed, despite the years that have passed.

Since early morning, Ma's voice has been echoing throughout the house. Her housework has begun. Now our days are passing under her care. Chacha, Bua and the others have slipped under her shadow. There is a new liveliness in the home, but discipline, too. Everyone is joyous. After regaining Ma, I have forgotten all my worries and doubts.

***

Papa is restless. He is involved in political work, but has sworn not to do a paid job in enslaved India. We do not have money. All we have are some envelopes given to us by our Sindhi friends. I know Papa will never spend this money; he will donate it to a fund. Satya Kaka is attached to a business. He will run the expenses of the house. For the time being, even without money, our hearts are happy and we are spirited; I desire to go fight again. Freedom is inevitable.

We spend these dark nights listening to stories of our time apart, stories of despair narrated by Ma. Our chatter continues wherever we are, even on a rickshaw ride. I have paraphrased some of Ma's stories here:

> From August 1945 onwards, the winds of a holocaust hovered over Japan.[55] The dropping of the atom bombs and the subsequent surrender of Japan by Emperor Hirohito came as a shock to everyone in Tokyo, including Ma.
>
> The emperor said: 'If we don't surrender now, then Japan will forever be erased from the map of the world. Our intention is to surrender so that a new Japan can be established.'

Most citizens of Japan collapsed in front of their radio sets. Ma, Tulu and our other Indian friends let a river of tears flow. What had the Japanese people not done for the victory of Nippon? Every Japanese life was one of struggle. Japanese women had sent everyone—their fathers, sons, husbands, brothers—into the battlefield, and they survived on nothing but rice water. All resources were sent to the southern war zones. Respite from war came as complete annihilation.

Ma and Tulu saw hundreds of people commit hara-kiri or suicide. Losing was unimaginable, an intolerable insult. They could not save their beloved Nippon. The only way they could apologize to their country, to their emperor, was through hara-kiri. Hundreds committed hara-kiri in front of the emperor's palace. Some friends of Ma and Papa's, a couple, committed suicide by piercing each other with a dagger.

After the desperate circumstances of the Japanese surrender, the American occupational army entered Japan like a flood. The Japanese were hungry, the national morale had collapsed. There was to be no more sacrifice, no more restraint. Japanese women, who were the models of sacrifice, began having dalliances with American soldiers; they wandered through the city, hand-in-hand, accepting gifts and help in return.

Meanwhile, imprisoned Japanese soldiers were released and returned home. They did not find comfort at home. Instead, they were met with anger and resentment. Hungry soldiers asking their mothers, wives and sisters for rice were refused, and told to flee; they were an embarrassment. How can losers return and demand food? 'Go work and feed yourself. There's no place for you here.'

For these soldiers, the doors to their homes were shut. Many began polishing shoes and doing odd jobs on the streets. Japanese women walked past them with their American friends; they paused to extend their legs and get their boots polished, while their American friends tossed money at the soldiers. The defeated Japanese soldiers tolerated even these insults.

Thousands of Japanese women left for America as brides. The Japanese people cannot live a life of defeat. They will rise, the winds of change will blow, and Japan's name will be glorified again. The spirits of those Japanese people who committed hara-kiri will return to the country and work towards its advancement.

***

Seeing the worsening situation in Japan, Ma opened a small shop in the corner of the house, selling various items she already possessed. She named the shop 'Manohari', a clever double entendre, meaning 'beautiful' in Hindi and 'things made of the needle' in Japanese.

After the end of the war, Japan, like the rest of the world, suffered from the winds of inflation. While everything was available in the market, the costs were prohibitive. Ma's shop benefited her immediate neighbours and the larger neighbourhood, too. She cut her sarees into thin strips, stitched them, and sold them as neckties. She also sold bedsheets, pillowcases, shoes, shirts, Java safflower oil and so on. All items in the shop were sold at a reasonable price; this was Ma's attempt at social service. She used whatever money she made to meet her household expenses. She kept a washerwoman from the neighbourhood as an assistant.

This woman was one of those who didn't let her husband back into the house after he returned from the war defeated. She also ate her meals at our house.

* * *

Soon after the Japanese surrender, news of Netaji's plane crash and subsequent death was broadcast on the radio in Japan. On the day of his death, there was a big typhoon in Tokyo and it rained a lot. That day, a framed photo of Netaji hanging from the wall of our Ogikubo house fell and its glass broke.

Ma had told Tulu: 'People in India believe that whenever a great spirit is born or dies, a big storm arrives and it rains a lot…'

And on the same day, our great Netaji left this world. On hearing the news broadcast on the radio in Japan, on 20 August, Ma fainted, and Tulu spent the entire day and night crying.

* * *

Carrying Netaji's ashes, Colonel Habib ur Rahman and Shri S.A. Ayer came to our house.[56] In Ma's words:

> At the beginning of September, a car suddenly stopped in front of our house. I went outside and saw Colonel Habib, Shri Ayer and Rama Murti standing there.[57]
>
> Habib Bhai said: 'Sister, I have brought Netaji. What should I do with him?'
>
> I said: 'For Netaji and for those who loved him, the door of the Sahay house is always open.'

They all came inside. Habib Bhai placed the urn in the showcase of our living room. We lit incense sticks and paid our respects.

I kept Habib Bhai and Shri Ayer safe in the room upstairs. At around midnight, I called a doctor from the neighbourhood who could treat Habib Bhai's burnt hand and face. I made him promise that he would keep this matter a complete secret because Netaji's own people were with us. The doctor fulfilled his duty.

On 18 September, we took Netaji to Renko-ji Temple. We placed chits of paper into Papa's hat. On the chits were the names of the forty trainee pilots. One chit was taken out, in which Cadet Nachiappan's name was written.[58] Nachiappan had the good fate of carrying Netaji's ashes to Renko-ji in his hands. At noon, our silent procession left home and we walked three kilometres to Renko-ji temple. I was with Tulu, Baby, Ashok, Ayer, Rama Murti, officers from the Japanese armed forces and some Japanese and Indian friends.

Renko-ji's main priest, Rev. Mochizuki, and six other priests performed the last rites together. I requested Rev. Mochizuki to keep Netaji's ashes safely till someone comes from India. He pledged that no one would be permitted to touch the urn. It would remain with him. Once that was decided, we all returned home peacefully.

For eighteen days prior to this, Netaji's ashes lay in a glass cupboard in the living room of our Tokyo house. It was kept next to framed photographs of Netaji. Every day, Tulu, I and the others lit incense sticks, and paid our respects. In those days, some of the forty-five trainee pilots—later known as the Tokyo Boys—were also staying with us. They supported Tulu and me in many different ways. They took turns and sat by Netaji's ashes at all times for ten days.

By this time, Colonel Habib and Shri Ayer had become well, and living secretly had become intolerable for them.

One day, they said to me: 'Sister, if you hear any kind of sound at night, you will not rise.'

I thought it strange. At around midnight my eyes opened. I somehow went upstairs. Colonel Habib was missing. I asked Shri Ayer: 'Where is Habib Bhai?'

Shri Ayer said: 'He has left.'

Where he went no one knew. A few days later, Shri Ayer also left and went to live in the hostel with the Tokyo Boys. One evening at around six thirty, Bimal, one of the Tokyo Boys, came running to us and said 'Colonel Habib is leaving. Come quickly.'

I limped to the crossroads and saw Colonel Habib standing there. I asked him: 'What's the matter, Habib Bhai?'

'They've come to take us. I am leaving; I will meet you in India.'

He said 'Jai Hind' and retreated to the boy's hostel. A little while later, American officers arrested Colonel Habib and Shri Ayer and sent them to India.

***

Words from Ma's mouth, narrating an incident told to her by Colonel Habib about the death of Netaji:

The plan was that we would come to Tokyo from Saigon, via Taihoku, and then head to Manchuria. But misfortune fell on us. On 18 August, the plane crashed soon after take-off and all of us seated within got injured. We narrowly escaped by jumping from the burning plane. Netaji was seated near the gasoline tank. His uniform caught fire as he was trying to exit and he started to burn. My hands and face also got burnt. I jumped from the plane and fell unconscious. When I regained consciousness, I found Netaji's half-burnt body near me.

He asked me: 'Habib, how are you?'

I respectfully said: 'I am fine. How are you?'

'I, perhaps, may not be able to live longer. When you go to India, please tell our countrymen that Subhas lived bravely and died bravely. India will soon be free. This is a certain future.'

He then became unconscious. A lorry came from the hospital and all the injured were loaded in. The Japanese doctors and staff tried their best to save Netaji, but at around 8.30 p.m., he took his last breath. I was seated by him and recited the namaaz aloud.

The Taihoku officials asked me: 'What shall we do with him?'

I responded that it's impossible to take Netaji anywhere. We should cremate him here in Taihoku.

A coffin was brought and Netaji was placed in it. Before the wooden lid was nailed shut, we (the doctors, officials, me and some others) saw him for the last time. We took Netaji to the crematorium. There, his body was placed on a slide and put into the electric chambers. The switch was turned on. Major Nagatomo, a Japanese army officer, and I returned to the military hospital. The next day, at 11 a.m., we went to the crematorium to collect Netaji's ashes. There, looking at Netaji's ashes, I was overcome with grief.

Major Nagatomo and I together placed his ashes and existence into a wooden box and nailed it shut. Major Nagatomo wrote 'Subhas Chandra Bose' in Japanese characters on one side of the box and I wrote it in English on the other. We tied the urn and took it to a Buddhist temple, Nishi Hongan-ji, and kept it safely there. We paid our respects there.

The ashes of General Isoda, who was on the same plane, and who died on the same day, were also placed there. His last rites were done simultaneously. When we next got a plane to Tokyo in September, we brought Netaji's ashes with us.

Saturday, 2 August 1947[59]

Time withers and memories are all that remain. More than two years have passed since I boarded a train from Tokyo to Kobe on that wintry morning, bidding farewell to life as I knew it. It is now 1947 and the air is heavy. It feels as though the grey monsoon clouds will reach down and grasp my fingers at any moment. We, the Sahays, have been finally reunited in our homeland. We are now standing on the precipice of Free India.

I am sometimes astonished that Ma–Papa sent their seventeen-year-old daughter to war under the leadership of Netaji. Both my parents are ardent believers of Gandhian thought; they followed the Gandhian way of life even when living in foreign countries. But they, like Netaji, were convinced that the draconian policies of the British had to be eliminated not by soft persuasion but by fighting, using arms.

Ma fully supported these activities with her invincible spirit and courage. It is this courage that enabled Mama-san to manage the household single-handedly when Papa was away for months and years at a time—first to Singapore, then other Southeast Asian countries. Difficulties increased as the war progressed and the Japanese war efforts shifted to the south. Japan is an island—millions of souls threaded together as one—but isolated from the rest of the world. As teenagers, it was difficult for us to fathom how Ma managed in such a chaotic atmosphere with no money and little food. But hunger did not bother us since we knew we were fighting for India's independence and the elimination of colonization from the whole of Asia. We were satisfied with two bowls of whey without salt, or one boiled potato, or, if we were lucky, a piece of boiled fish.

I was young and impatient when I joined the RJR; I yearned to pick up a rifle and march straight to Imphal. But the war was such that even reaching Bangkok for my training to commence took several months. Little did I realize that the journey was as important as the destination. Faces of those whose paths crossed mine still flash before my eyes. There are those whom I hope to meet again, and those whom I know I will meet in another life. They lived and fought for a higher ideal—an ideal I will try my best to emulate.

In August 1945, I was a newly commissioned lieutenant in the Rani of Jhansi Regiment of the Indian National Army. I was anxious and eager to reach the frontline as soon as possible, but it was not in my fate to look the enemy in the eye. My rifle did not fire any bullets, my bayonet did not slash the arteries of any enemies. An entire organization—a structure that Netaji, Papa and countless other brave patriots had built over the years—fell apart in a matter of weeks. First, with the atom bombs of Hiroshima and Nagasaki. Then the Japanese surrender. Then the death of Netaji. My war ended before it began.

War is silence. War is doubt. War is not knowing. After the Japanese surrender, I had no news of Papa for several months.

Then I learnt that he was alive but imprisoned, a death sentence swinging over his head like a pendulum. Satya Kaka had become a ghost, traces of him appearing and disappearing from the depths of the jungle. Ma, Tulu, Baby, and Ashok—they were radiant in my memories, but I did not know if they had survived the bombs. If they had survived, I knew their lives in Tokyo would be a struggle—harsh winters, no food, bent bones.

When we returned to India in 1946, my emotions were as uncertain as the times. I had been reunited with my motherland, but without Mama-san. I was home, but I yearned for Ogikubo—my family, my friends, my old neighbourhood. In my dreams, I had tasted the moist earth of India and now I walked on her soil. But not freely. India was not free, and I gradually realized I, too, was shackled by a new set of customs and superstitions. The deeper we entered India, the more rigid the rules became.

As we met the leaders who had sacrificed everything to free India, I felt inadequate. I sang '*Shubh sukh chain*' before crowds of dreamers, but I felt like I didn't belong. What had I done for the country? Papa and Satya Kaka tried to reassure me, but I could never let go of that unnerving feeling. Was I a patriot or a charlatan? Who was I? A homesick teenager who only wanted her mother? Or an eighteen-year-old who had sworn to fight till her dying breath? What had I achieved? I felt like I was living a dual life—sometimes a quiet Japanese bookworm and, at other times, a headstrong Indian patriot. Somewhere and nowhere in between.

The world became a brighter place when Ma, Tulu, Baby and Ashok returned to India. I felt as though I had been reunited with a missing piece of myself, a missing piece of my soul.

It is now August 1947 and the Indian Independence Act has been passed by the British Parliament. India will finally be free. Our dreams have come true, but we are shadowed by uncertainty.

The British have saved their worst injury for the end—the amputation of our Mother India. But I know that we, the patriots of Free India, will overcome this pain, too. We will walk on the path set before us by Netaji. It will rain happiness and peace, and we will awaken to our destiny. The future is ours. Jai Hind!

AUTHOR'S NOTE

by Lt Bharati 'Asha' Sahay Choudhry

The year 1928: the quiet of noon. The snow-laced land of Kobe. And, on Japanese soil, the daughter of an Indian family flutters her eyelashes for the first time. Her father, Anand, is ecstatic and Sati, the girl's mother, glances out of the window at the white world enveloping them. She feels a warmth permeate through her. Admiring the child from head to toe, they are filled with hope, 'Asha', for India, 'Bharat'. Then laughingly, they name the child Asha and Bharati, and shower her with blessings.

* * *

I was born at Konan Hospital in the middle of the magical Rokko-san hills. I did not cry as I left my mother's womb; I was a blue baby. The German doctor treating me put his mouth to mine and sucked the phlegm out of my lungs. It was only then that my cries of life could be heard echoing through the hospital. He saved my life before it began.

As a consequence of my parents' endeavours in Japan, my early education began in Japanese schools, where my friends respectfully called me Asha-san. I finished my primary and secondary education in Kobe, and then my parents sent me to Tokyo's reputed Showa Kojo College (now Showa Women's University) for further studies.

During this time, the Second World War commenced; Papa and Satya Kaka, my father's younger brother, travelled south from Japan to assist in India's freedom struggle. Then, Netaji Subhas Chandra Bose arrived in Tokyo, and I, too, followed in their footsteps, joining the RJR and rising to the rank of a lieutenant.

I have been writing in my diary since my early childhood. Bombs may fall, typhoons may swirl—yet I cannot sleep without writing in my diary. I originally wrote this diary in Japanese on fragments of paper and notebooks of inferior quality, the only materials available during the war. For the people of my nation, I have compiled and translated my diary into Hindi. These words are my small contribution to India.

While reflecting on the years gone by, another thought strikes me—nothing I have done would have been successful without the blessings of my parents. Our parents are truly another form of the Almighty. If the generations after can understand this truth, I will consider my labours fruitful.

FOREWORD TO THE HINDI EDITION

by Anand Mohan Sahay

It gives me great pleasure to know that my soul, Asha, has gathered her experiences of the last world war in the form of a book.

During and before the war, we resided in Japan, where we had an uncommon and unique opportunity to work for India's independence. Asha was also witness to these experiences.

In 1943, Netaji Subhas Chandra Bose reached Tokyo from Germany, and established the Azad Hind Government and the Indian National Army across East Asia. The Rani of Jhansi Regiment also became a part of this. Asha voluntarily wanted to be included in the regiment and requested Netaji for permission. Netaji admitted her as a cadet to a training camp in Bangkok.

The war transformed Asha from being a delicate, emotional girl into someone who was spirited—a girl who could face any fires, any storms. I witnessed this change in her as a neutral observer.

Writing the details of those unprecedented historical times and presenting them to readers as a book is essential and will prove advantageous to the country, too. Whatever Asha has written is based on her experiences; it is the truth and reality. It has not been influenced by the politics of the present era.

Today, we hear the voices of separatism within the country—due to language, due to caste, and so on. In such delicate times, Netaji's immutable patriotism and nationalism serve as a reminder for the country—a message that unity is not just necessary, but obligatory. Netaji entwined the members of the Azad Hind Government and the INA with the holy threads of unity. The lack of a hero like him is being felt by all lovers of India. Under Netaji's shadow, we were all citizens of India. There were no other nouns, no other divisions. For India, we were ready to sacrifice everything.

The publication of a book like this, based on the ideals of Netaji, is timely. There can be no doubt that feelings of patriotism will arise in a new generation. For this reason, Asha is worthy of our immense praise and gratitude.

I have complete faith that readers will benefit from this book, and will be motivated to serve and uplift the nation. Jai Hind.

TRANSLATOR'S NOTE

by Tanvi Srivastava

Seventy-five years have passed since Asha-san last wrote in this diary. She is now ninety-four years old, a proud citizen of Free India. She lives in Patna with her son, Sanjay, and daughter-in-law, Ratna.

I first met Asha-san, my husband's grandmother, on a bright winter's morning in 2013; she strutted into the dining room carrying a heavy saucepan of rice, refusing all help, barking at those who dared to offer it. I was about to be introduced to the art and ceremony of sushi making. She laid out the ingredients with precision: a bowl of salted water, three bamboo mats, several sheets of nori, finely sliced vegetables, a sharp knife and a mound of vinegared rice, still steaming. She then put on her reading glasses and pinched the short-grained rice between her fingers to see if it had cooked fully. Several rows of vegetarian maki rolls soon appeared before us. The untidy edges were chopped off and kept aside (for the household help, she whispered). With the rice that remained, Dadi delicately shaped a triangle. Onigiri, she said, inserting a heart of shudderingly sour pickled plum. I now realize that this is war food—with roots deep in the darkest days of the Second World War. When Japan was blockaded and starved by both the Allied powers and its own leaders. When there was nothing left to eat but rice, and that too, barely a fistful per person. Add some powdered sugar and grind it to a paste to make a dessert. Serve it with miso soup or a chicken broth, and it is a meal worthy of royalty.

Since marrying her grandson, I've heard Dadi's war stories in passing; fleeting tales that appear without warning. She must lunge forward and grab these stories by the throat, wrestling to bring them to life; else, they will forever disappear. The fog of war has gone and now the fog of memory is all that remains. And the memories are astonishing: it's the story of an Indian girl growing up in Kobe and Tokyo before the war, living a life steeped in Japanese culture, nationalism and ethos. It's the story of how ordinary men and women became soldiers, sacrificing their lives for the notion of 'Mother India', even though they had never stepped on her soil. It's the story of the Indian National Army, of alliances, and how fate, rather than men (or women), decided where things would begin and how they would end. And lastly, it's the coming-of-age story of a seventeen-year-old who leaves her home and family to discover herself as a woman.

Translating something as personal as a diary can be a source of discomfort. Especially when the author is someone known: a free-willed woman who does not shy away from proudly saluting military officers as colleagues, a loud 'Jai Hind' on her lips. However, Dadi has been supportive throughout the process. As she physically weakens, she is glad that Sanjay and I have taken on this endeavour. Not many people have a mother or grandmother or great-grandmother who fought for India's freedom, traversing the vast canvas of East and Southeast Asia in the footsteps of Netaji. I am lucky to be able to share her story with my children and I hope you can share it with your children, too.

Notes on the diary

Asha-san's original diary was written in Japanese during the Second World War. She wrote it in pencil on scraps of paper and frayed notebooks, whatever material was available during the war. Sadly, the original Japanese diary has been lost.

Asha-san translated the Japanese version of the diary into Hindi with the assistance of her parents and her Hindi professor on her return to India. It was first published in a serialized manner in the Hindi weekly magazine *Dharmyug* from May to July 1973. The entries were later compiled into a book titled *Asha-san Ki Subhas Diary* published by Shankar Dayal Singh of Parijat Prakashan in Patna.

There are only a few copies of the Hindi translation extant—two of which are in Asha-san's house in Patna. Sanjay can be credited for making sure the words in this diary are not lost to time. He informally republished the book in 2011, after getting it re-typed by a Tamilian whose first language was not Hindi. Some typographical errors crept into the document at this stage. For example, 'India' (Bharat) was mistyped as 'rice' (bhaat), causing some amusement. Another example is the Japanese word 'tonarigumi' mistyped as 'vonari gumi'. Nonetheless, the idiom of the original Japanese has not been lost in the Hindi translation, especially in the early chapters when Japan is closer to Asha-san's heart—its people, its weather, its seasons. It is unsurprising that I greatly enjoyed the challenge this book posed. I, too, misinterpreted some words. For example, 'Indojin' means 'Indian people' in Japanese, but I incorrectly assumed the book was referring to 'Indochin', or Indochina in Southeast Asia. It was only when I heard Asha-san speak much later that I realized my mistake. I have done my best to decipher these errors, but I am certain there are more that will be uncovered once this book is published.

Notes on the translation

I was inspired to take on this project after reading an article by Jhumpa Lahiri, where she calls translation a form of 'literary apprenticeship'. It was my fortune that Asha-san's Hindi diary was waiting for me on my bookshelf. In the process of translating this work, I have learnt much about Asha-san, her writing style, as well as the English language. English can sometimes be a listless language; to overcome this, I have taken some literary licence, hoping to transfer what I know of Asha-san—her love for nature, her Japanese ethos of perfection and etiquette—onto these pages. The changes or additions I have made are minor and are not factual in nature; they simply serve to make the narrative flow in a seamless manner.

Asha-san attempted an English translation of the Hindi diary several years ago. While this translation was never completed, she did add certain supplementary information—for example, the name of the hostel she and Tulu were sent to in 1943—in the portions she did translate. She also wrote down some memories in 2018 while visiting us in Bangalore. I have incorporated this supplementary information into this version of the diary.

Notes on time

It is remarkable that events that took place three quarters of a century ago are still alive in Asha-san's memory. However, readers will notice that there are some inconsistencies, especially when it comes to time. The dates mentioned in this diary differ slightly from the Hindi diary, as well as from events of the period. The war was a time of turbulence—and the chaos that ensued also affected memories. History in such turbulent times is not static but constantly in flow—from the eyes to the brain, from memory to paper, melting and morphing as it is processed and reiterated. In my research for this book, I discovered several conflicting sources. For example, Hugh Toye's *The Springing Tiger* and the Government of India's Ministry of Information and Broadcasting's *Selected Speeches of Subhas Chandra Bose* state different dates for the same event: a speech by Netaji on the treatment meted out to INA prisoners of war was broadcast from Bangkok either on 30 May 1945 or on 14 June 1945, depending on which source you choose to believe. Recorded history can be fallible, perhaps due to typographical errors or due to fading memories.

The dates in this book are based on the dates mentioned in the Hindi diary republished in 2011. Corrections have been made for typographical errors and to maintain chronological continuity. An example of a correction made is when Asha-san and Tulu meet the INA cadets (the Tokyo Boys) in their home, according to the Hindi diary, in 1943. However, the Tokyo Boys only arrived in Japan in 1944. The diary mentions the date—16 July 1943—as a Sunday. However, 16 July 1943 was a Friday. On the other hand, 16 July 1944 was a Sunday, and I have taken the liberty to amend the date in this publication.

The dates in the Hindi diary become more inconsistent from February 1945 onwards. This is around the time Asha-san leaves Tokyo to join the Rani of Jhansi Regiment. Some dates are repeated, and the chronology often breaks. This is true in all versions of the Hindi diary—from that published in *Dharmyug* in 1973 to the 2011 version. I have taken the liberty of amending the dates so they broadly follow a chronological sequence. In the instances where I am unsure of a date, I use broader terms such as 'a few days later' or simply club the entry into a range of months, such as 'October–November'. I would like to state that while the dates may not be exact, they do fall into the correct seasons, and this is the mechanism Asha-san uses to remember dates—whether it was snowing or whether the rains had arrived.

CHARACTER SKETCHES[60]

Papa (Anand Mohan Sahay)

Papa was born in Bhagalpur, a district of Bihar, on 10 September 1898. He became a nationalist early in life, working closely with leaders such as Dr Rajendra Prasad, Mahatma Gandhi, and later, Rash Behari Bose in Japan. He helped set up several branches of the Indian Independence League across Asia. These branches would become a central network for the Indian National Army—a source of both soldiers and funds. He encouraged members of India's diaspora in several Asian countries, including Japan, China, Manchuria, Thailand, Burma, Vietnam and Hong Kong, to unite against British imperialism.

Upon Netaji's arrival in Japan, Papa became his political adviser and joined the cabinet of the Provisional Government of

Azad Hind as secretary (with ministerial rank). He was closely associated with the development of the Azad Hind governance structure and its administration in the Andaman and Nicobar Islands, as well as in Burma.

Papa made Southeast Asia the main centre of his political activities. He was arrested at the end of the Second World War and released several months later. Upon his return to India, he shared inspiring stories about the bravery of INA soldiers. An estimated 37,000 soldiers out of a total strength of 60,000—more than 60 per cent—were martyred, leading to immense public outcry across India, followed by mutinies in the armed forces, including the Royal Indian Navy uprising of 1946.[61] The efforts of the Azad Hind Government and the sacrifices of the INA soldiers hastened the end of British rule in India.

From 1950 onwards, Papa served as India's High Commissioner to the British West Indies, Madagascar, Mauritius, Vietnam and Thailand. Upon retirement, he worked in the field of women's education till the end of his life. His memoirs were published in a book titled *Stirring Times: An Autobiography of a Nationalist*. He passed away in 1991.

Ma (Sati Sen Sahay)

Ma was born on 27 September 1903 to Nalini Sen and Sophiya Sen. Unfortunately, her mother died soon after Ma was born. Ma lived with her maternal aunt till my Dadu, Nalini, remarried. His second wife, Didima (Urmila Devi), was the sister of the famous barrister and Congress leader from Calcutta, Chittaranjan Das. Ma shifted to Didima's home at the age of seven. Dadu and Didima had a son, Ma's stepbrother, my Mama, Jiten Sen, who later joined the *Statesman* and became a well-known journalist.

Ma and Mama were educated in Calcutta; she was a rebellious girl who often got into trouble with the European nuns at her convent school. She insisted on singing the British national anthem as '*God* Shave *the King*', blaming her Bengali accent for the mispronunciation. Her independent spirit flowered when she was admitted to Rabindranath Tagore's Visva-Bharati University in Santiniketan, which inculcated in her a love for nature, the arts and nationalism.

Papa and Ma got married in 1927, on the first day of the Bengali New Year (Poila Boisakh) in Calcutta. They set sail for Japan soon after. While Papa was spreading the message of freedom across Asia, Ma was left with the responsibility of running the household with a meagre income. She also supported Papa's work for India's freedom from afar. She helped publish the English–Japanese journal, *Voice of India,* and was instrumental in spreading the message of nationalism among Indian women. Ma also designed the currency notes of the Azad Hind Government, using the fine-arts skills she had acquired at Santiniketan.

The war years were especially difficult when food was in short supply and rationing was in force. Ma suffered from severe arthritis, which progressively worsened because of Japan's cold winter. Every time the air-raid sirens went off, Ma had to be helped into the trenches. Despite this, she raised the spirits of others by singing patriotic songs in Japanese and Bengali. After Japan surrendered, she gave shelter to the forty-five INA cadets who had nowhere to go. Barracks were built behind our home in Ogikubo, and Ma and Tulu provided them with meals, despite the severe scarcity the entire country was facing.

Towards the end of her life, despite being bedridden, she never stopped reading or writing. Her compositions were published frequently in the Bengali magazine, *Desh.* Ma passed away in December 1976.

Satya Kaka (Satyadev Sahay)

Satyadev Sahay—Satto to friends and family—was born on 29 September 1911. He was as handsome as his eldest brother—slim, tall and swarthy. Kaka convinced his sister-in-law, Sati Sahay, to bring him over to Japan to join the freedom struggle. Ma sold some ornaments to buy his passage to the country. He landed in Kobe at the age of nineteen in 1930. He quickly learnt Japanese and revived Papa's neglected trading firm, earning an income for the family.

Kaka joined the INA in 1943. Accepted into the nascent intelligence and espionage wing by Netaji, he was given dangerous missions to handle, though very little is known about this aspect of his life. S.A. Ayer mentions that Satyadev Sahay was always following them in Malaya, Burma and other countries.[62] We often asked him to share his stories, but he only smiled in response. He spoke about two occasions: one was an incident involving a traitor—an informant of the British—who had to be neutralized. An accident was planned and executed. The other was when he staged the bombing of a major public meeting in Rangoon. Many British dignitaries and army generals had gathered to address a crowd in a football stadium, and Kaka had been tasked to ensure the event did not happen. Bombs went off as soon as the dignitaries arrived, and people ran helter-skelter, effectively stopping the meeting.

When he learnt that Papa was imprisoned in Singapore's Pearl Hill Prison, Kaka made friends with the warden, and kept Papa supplied with news and food. He remained underground for several months, hiding from the Allied forces who were keen to interrogate him. After his encounter with Nehruji in Singapore, he was arrested and kept in custody for two months.

After independence, Kaka started trading in textiles with Japan; Bhagalpur was famous for its silk, and he got the government of

Japan to set up the Silk Institute here. He married Madhavi Sahay, the daughter of Professor Prasad, head of the Hindi department in Tribhuvan University, Kathmandu. He died at the age of sixty-seven in May 1978.

Tulu (Riziya Sahay Teelock)

Tulu was born in Kobe on 29 December 1929. She was named 'Riziya' by Shri Futehally, a friend of Papa's, who, in turn, named Futehally's daughter 'Jaya'. This is an example of the unity prevalent between Hindus and Muslims in those days.

During the war, Tulu was the main support of our family, especially during the years when Papa, Kaka and I were away. The situation was difficult and Tulu, only sixteen then, became responsible for Ma when she was sick, while caring for Baby and Ashok. She foraged for food, fuel and medicines with courage and ingenuity both during and after the war.

In July 1947, Tulu returned to India with Ma and the others. She learnt Hindi and finished her Intermediate College from Allahabad. Soon, she was travelling across the world: Papa was sent as a diplomat to various countries, and Tulu served as hostess rather than Ma, who was not in good health.

Tulu married Dr Boodhun Teelock of Mauritius in Bhagalpur in 1955. Tulu had a magnetic personality, forever drawing people to her. She spent a lot of energy on social work and promoting sports in Mauritius. She passed away in June 2004.

Baby (Sumona Sahay Varma)

Baby was born on 19 May 1932. After returning from Japan, she studied in Mahadevi Varma Vidyapeeth and Sundarvati University. Soon after, she married Shri Vidyashankar Varma, the chief engineer in a reputed firm. Baby is a skilled practitioner of ikebana. She lives in Patna not too far away from me. We meet often, reminiscing about life and our years in Japan.

Ashok (Ashok Mohan Sahay)

Ashok was born on 1 August 1936. Upon return to India, he studied at St Xavier's School, Patna, and St Stephen's College, Delhi. He worked for the *Hindustan Times* as a member of the editorial team. Ashok passed away in 2020.

***

Members of the Azad Hind Government, the Indian National Army and the Indian Independence League mentioned in this book:

Ayer, S.A. – Minister of publicity and propaganda in the Provisional Government of Azad Hind. Born in Tamil Nadu in 1898, Ayer was a journalist who moved to Thailand in 1941 as a special correspondent for Reuters. A year later, he joined the IIL and soon became a close associate of Netaji. Ayer is the author of two books, *Story of the INA* and *Unto Him a Witness: The Story of Netaji Subhas Chandra Bose*.

Bai, Janaki Fateh Singh (Lt) – Asha's platoon commander in the Rani of Jhansi Regiment. Born in 1922 in Sabak Bernam, Malaya, Janaki Bai grew up in a large coconut estate where her father worked as an assistant manager. She first heard Netaji at a public rally in Singapore and joined the RJR training camp soon after. After the war, she became a schoolteacher and lived in Malaysia.

Bashir, S.M. – An Indian merchant and a member of the IIL, Burma. Sheikh Mohammad Bashir owned a rubber factory in

Kamayut on the outskirts of Rangoon and assisted the Azad Hind Government in raising funds.

Bhatia, Ved Prakash (Lt) – Lieutenant, INA.

Bhonsle, J.K. (Maj. Gen.) – Chief of staff, INA. A graduate of both the Prince of Wales Royal Indian Military College in Dehradun and the Royal Military College in Sandhurst, Bhonsle was the highest-ranking officer of the INA. He originally served in the 5th Mahratta Light Infantry of the British Indian Army. After Singapore fell, he was one of the first to volunteer for the first INA under Captain Mohan Singh. After the war, he served in the Government of India as deputy minister, Ministry of Rehabilitation.

Bhowmick, Anjuli (Rani) – One of the youngest members of the RJR, Anjuli was only twelve when she enlisted with her sister, Shanti. Her father, Dhirendra Chandra Bhowmick, was a supporter of Netaji and the Forward Bloc; he was eager to join the INA but ill health prevented him from doing so. Anjuli and Shanti seized this opportunity to volunteer for the RJR.

Bhowmick, Shanti (Rani) – Anjuli Bhowmick's elder sister, Shanti, joined the RJR at the age of fourteen. Both sisters were born in Dacca, but moved to Seremban, Malaya, at a young age when their father joined a rubber plantation as an assistant manager. She was later known as Shanti Majumdar.

Bose, Rash Behari – An Indian revolutionary wanted by British intelligence since 1912 for an assassination attempt on the then viceroy and governor general of India, Lord Hardinge. Bose fled to Japan in 1915, became a Japanese citizen, and continued to struggle for India's freedom. He chaired the Tokyo and Bangkok Conferences held in 1942 and was the first president of the IIL. He handed over the leadership of the

IIL, and its subordinate, the INA, to Netaji Subhas Chandra Bose in October 1943.

Chatterji, A.C. (Maj. Gen.) – Finance minister in the Provisional Government of Azad Hind. When Singapore fell, he was the most senior officer of the Indian Medical Service. In 1944, he was appointed as governor designate of liberated territories (governor of Burma and Manipur) and, in 1945, he served as foreign minister of the Azad Hind Government.

Choudhry, L.P. (Dr) – An Indian nationalist and medical doctor, he founded the All-Calcutta and All-Bengal Medical Students Union. A neighbour of the Sahays in Bihar, he married Bharati 'Asha' Sahay Choudhry in 1949. They had two children, Praveer and Sanjay.

Das, Debnath – Adviser to the Provisional Government of Azad Hind. Das was the founding secretary of the Indian National Council, a nationalist organization founded in Bangkok in 1941. He later became general secretary of the IIL branch in Thailand. He was closely associated with the Sahay family and lived in Calcutta after the war.

Dasan, D. (Capt.) – One of the forty-five INA cadets (Tokyo Boys) sent to Japan for training, Dasan was selected to join the Imperial Japanese Army Air Academy. After the war, he obtained a pilot's licence and taught at the Patna Flying Club. He later retired from Air India as a senior administrator and spent the rest of his life in Chennai.

Dasgupta, Pratima (Rani) – Lieutenant, RJR.

Dhillon, Gurbaksh Singh (Col.) – A graduate of the Indian Military Academy, Dehradun, Dhillon was commissioned to the 1st Battalion of the 14th Punjab Regiment of the British Indian

Army. After the fall of Singapore, Dhillon joined the first INA, but could not be appointed to any role due to an illness. Later, under Netaji, he was appointed commander of the 4th Guerrilla Regiment, the Nehru Brigade. Dhillon, along with Shah Nawaz Khan and Prem Sehgal, was accused of waging war against the British Emperor in the historic Red Fort trials of 1946. After the war, he wrote an autobiography titled *From My Bones* (New Delhi: Aryan Books International, 2002).

Hasan, Abid (Maj.) – A trusted aide of Netaji, who accompanied him on his hazardous submarine journey from Germany to Japan in 1943. After the war, he joined the Indian Foreign Service, and served as Ambassador to Denmark and Egypt. He wrote a book about his time with the INA called *The Men from Imphal* (Calcutta: Netaji Research Bureau, 1971).

Karmakar, Somendra (Cadet) – One of the forty-five INA cadets (Tokyo Boys) sent to Japan for training, Karmakar's father was an engineer with the municipal corporation of Singapore when he joined the INA in 1943. He was one of the ten cadets selected to join the Imperial Japanese Army Air Academy. After the war, Karmakar lived near Jamshedpur, Bihar.

Khan, D.M. – He was initially appointed as secretary, Social and Welfare Department, IIL, under Rash Behari Bose. Later, under Netaji, he was also assigned the Housing and Transport Department. He served as an adviser to the Provisional Government of Azad Hind.

Khan, Shah Nawaz (Maj. Gen.) – One of the representatives of the armed forces (INA) to the Provisional Government of Azad Hind, Khan was a graduate of the Prince of Wales Royal Indian Military College and served in the 14th Punjab Regiment. After the fall of Singapore, he served as commander of the 1st Guerrilla

Regiment of the INA—the Subhas Brigade—which fought in the Arakan and on the Indian frontier in 1944. Shah Nawaz Khan, along with Gurbaksh Singh Dhillon and Prem Sehgal, was accused of waging war against the British Emperor in the historic Red Fort trials of 1946. He later served as a minister in the Government of India.

Kiani, Mohammed Zaman (Maj. Gen.) – One of the representatives of the armed forces (INA) to the Provisional Government of Azad Hind, Kiani was a graduate of the Indian Military Academy and served in the 1st Battalion of the 14th Punjab Regiment of the British Indian Army. After the fall of Singapore, he joined the first INA as chief of general staff. On the arrival of Netaji, he took command of the first division, leading the Subhas Brigade, the Gandhi Brigade and the Azad Brigade to fight in the Arakan, Tamu, Palel and Kohima in 1944. He was later appointed general secretary to the War Council. Following the partition of India, he became a citizen of Pakistan.

Loganathan, A.D. (Maj. Gen.) – One of the representatives of the armed forces (INA) to the Provisional Government of Azad Hind, Loganathan was an officer of the Indian Medical Service. He served as director of medical services in the first INA and was one of the delegates of the Bangkok Conference. Under Netaji, he was appointed as governor of the Andaman and Nicobar Islands, and later took command of the INA during its surrender in 1945. He was acquitted in the Red Fort trials and retired to Bangalore after the war.

Murti, Munga Rama – Head of the Indian Independence League, Tokyo.

Nachiappan (Cadet) – One of the forty-five INA cadets (Tokyo Boys) sent to Japan for training as an officer at the Imperial Japanese Army Academy.

Naraindas, B. – An Indian merchant who was a member of the IIL.

Navarednam, Ponnammah Esther (Rani) – Originally from Ceylon, the Navarednam sisters had recently moved to Ipoh, Malaya, with their widowed mother where they heard a speech given by Netaji at a large rally. Thoroughly inspired, Ponnammah joined the RJR at the age of eighteen. After the war and post retirement, Ponnammah moved to the United States.

Navarednam, Rasammah Naomi (Rani) – Rasammah joined the RJR at the age of sixteen. In 2006, she published her memoirs with Aruna Gopinath in a book titled *Footprints on the Sands of Time, Rasammah Bhupalan: A Life of Purpose* (Kuala Lumpur: Arkib Negara Malaysia, 2007). She lived in Kuala Lampur after the war.

Rahman, Habib ur (Col.) – Assistant chief of staff, INA. Rahman was a graduate of the Indian Military Academy and served in the 1st Battalion of the 14th Punjab Regiment of the British Indian Army. After the fall of Singapore, he served as the adjutant general in the first INA before becoming a trusted officer of Netaji. He was the only INA officer to accompany Netaji on his ill-fated flight to Tokyo. After the partition of India, he became a citizen of Pakistan.

Sarkar, A.N. – Legal adviser to the Provisional Government of Azad Hind.

Sharma, Raghunath (Pandit) – President of the IIL in Bangkok. Pandit Sharma arrived in Thailand in 1923 and returned to India in 1970. He founded the Hindu Samaj in Bangkok.

Singh, Ishar – Adviser to the Provisional Government of Azad Hind.

Thakur, Ram Singh (Capt.) – A member of the INA noted for composing the music to '*Shubh sukh chain*', '*Kadam kadam barhaye ja*', and '*Subhasji*'.

Thivy, John A. – A Malaysian–Indian lawyer who served as an adviser to the Provisional Government of Azad Hind. Thivy also served as the vice president of the IIL. He was arrested after the Japanese surrender and released several years later. He lived in Malaysia till his death in 1959.

Xavier, Emily (Rani) – A member of the RJR, recruited from Burma.

PROCLAMATION OF THE PROVISIONAL GOVERNMENT OF AZAD HIND (FREE INDIA)

The following proclamation was read by Netaji Subhas Chandra Bose in front of a gathering of Indians at Cathay Cinema, Singapore, on 21 October 1943:[63]

> After their first defeat at the hands of the British in 1757 in Bengal, the Indian people fought an uninterrupted series of hard and bitter battles over a stretch of one hundred years. The history of this period teems with examples of unparalleled heroism and self-sacrifice. And, in the pages of that history, the names of Siraj-ud-doula and Mohanlal of Bengal, Haider Ali, Tippu Sultan and Vellu Tampi of South India, Appa Sahib Bhonsle and Peshwa Baji Rao of Maharashtra, the Begums of Oudh, Sardar Shyam Singh Atariwala of Punjab and last, but not least, Rani

Lakshmibai of Jhansi, Tantia Tope, Maharaj Kunwar Singh of Dumraon and Nana Sahib—among others—the names of all these warriors are for ever engraved in letters of gold. Unfortunately for us, our forefathers did not at first realise that the British constituted a grave threat to the whole of India and they did not therefore put up a united front against the enemy. Ultimately, when the Indian people were roused to the reality of the situation, they made a concerted move—and under the flag of Bahadur Shah, in 1857, they fought their last war as free men. In spite of a series of brilliant victories in the early stages of this war, ill-luck and faulty leadership gradually brought about their final collapse and subjugation. Nevertheless, such heroes as the Rani of Jhansi, Tantia Tope, Kunwar Singh and Nana Sahib live like eternal stars in the nation's memory to inspire us to greater deeds of sacrifice and valour.

Forcibly disarmed by the British after 1857 and subjected to terror and brutality, the Indian people lay prostrate for a while—but with the birth of the Indian National Congress in 1885, there came a new awakening. From 1885 till the end of the last World War, the Indian people, in their endeavour to recover their lost liberty, tried all possible methods—namely, agitation and propaganda, boycott of British goods, terrorism and sabotage—and finally, armed revolution. But all these efforts failed for a time. Ultimately, in 1920, when the Indian people, haunted by a sense of failure, were groping for a new method, Mahatma Gandhi came forward with the new weapon of non-co-operation and civil disobedience.

For two decades thereafter the Indian people went through a phase of intense patriotic activity. The message of freedom was carried to every Indian home. Through personal example, people were taught to suffer, to sacrifice and to die in the cause of freedom. From the centre to the remotest villages, the people were knit together into one political organisation. Thus, the Indian people not only recovered their political consciousness, but became a political entity once again. They could now speak with one voice and strive with one will for one common goal. From 1937 to 1939, through the work of the Congress Ministries in eight provinces, they gave proof of their readiness and their capacity to administer their own affairs.

Thus on the eve of the present World War, the stage was set for the final struggle for India's liberation. During the course of this war, Germany, with the help of her Allies has dealt shattering blows to our enemy in Europe—while Nippon with the help of her Allies has inflicted a knockout blow to our enemy in East Asia. Favoured by a most happy combination of circumstances, the Indian people today have a wonderful opportunity for achieving their national emancipation.

For the first time in recent history, Indians abroad have also been politically roused and united in one organisation. They are not only thinking and feeling in tune with their countrymen at home, but are also marching in step with them, along the path to Freedom. In East Asia, in particular, over two million Indians are now organised as one solid phalanx, inspired by the slogan of "Total Mobilisation." And in front of them stand the serried ranks of India's Army of Liberation, with the slogan "Onward to Delhi" on their lips.

Having goaded Indians to desperation by its hypocrisy and having driven them to starvation and death by plunder and loot, British rule in India has forfeited the goodwill of the Indian people altogether and is now living a precarious existence. It needs but a flame to destroy the last vestige of that unhappy rule. To light that flame is the task of India's Army of Liberation. Assured of the enthusiastic support of the civil population at home and also of a large section of British Indian Army and backed by gallant and invincible allies abroad, but relying in the first instance on its own strength, India's Army of Liberation is confident of fulfilling its historic role.

Now that the dawn of freedom is at hand, it is the duty of the Indian people to set up a Provisional Government of their own, and launch the last struggle under the banner of that Government. But with all the Indian leaders in prison and the people at home totally disarmed—it is not possible to set up a Provisional Government within India or to launch an armed struggle under the aegis of that Government. It is, therefore, the duty of the Indian Independence League in East Asia, supported by all patriotic Indians at home and abroad, to undertake this task—the task of setting up a Provisional Government of Azad Hind (Free India) and of conducting the last fight for freedom, with the help of the Army of Liberation (that is, the Azad Hind Fauj or the Indian National Army) organised by the League.

Having been constituted as the Provisional Government of Azad Hind by the Indian Independence League in East Asia, we enter upon our duties with a full sense of the responsibility that has devolved on us. We pray that Providence may bless our work and our struggle for the emancipation of our Motherland. And we hereby pledge our lives and the lives of our comrades in arms to the cause of her freedom, of her welfare, and her exaltation among the nations of the world.

It will be the task of the Provisional Government to launch and to conduct the struggle that will bring about the expulsion of the British and of their allies from the soil of India. It will then be the task of the Provisional Government to bring about the establishment of a permanent National Government of Azad Hind constituted in accordance with the will of the Indian people and enjoying their confidence. After the British and their allies are overthrown and until a Permanent National Government of Azad Hind is set up on Indian soil, the Provisional Government will administer the affairs of the country in trust for the Indian people.

The Provisional Government is entitled to, and hereby claims, the allegiance of every Indian. It guarantees religious liberty, as well as equal rights and equal opportunities to all its citizens. It declares its firm resolve to pursue the happiness and prosperity of the whole nation and of all its parts, cherishing all the children of the nation equally and transcending all the differences cunningly fostered by an alien government in the past.

In the name of God, in the name of bygone generations who have welded the Indian people into one nation and in the name of the dead heroes who have bequeathed to us a tradition of heroism and self-sacrifice—we call upon the Indian people to rally round our banner and to strike for India's freedom. We call upon them to launch the final struggle against the British and all their allies in India and to prosecute that struggle with valour and perseverance and with full faith in final victory—until the enemy is expelled from Indian soil and the Indian people are once again a Free Nation.

Signed on behalf of the Provisional Government of Azad Hind.

SUBHAS CHANDRA BOSE *(Head of the State, Prime Minister and Minister for War and Foreign Affairs);*

CAPT. MRS. LAKSHMI *(Women's Organisation);*

S. A. AYER *(Publicity and Propaganda);*

LT.-COL. A. C. CHATTERJI *(Finance);*

LT.-COL. AZIZ AHMED, LT.-COL. N. S. BHAGAT, LT.-COL. J. K. BHONSLE, LT.-COL. GULZARA SINGH, LT.-COL. M. Z. KIANI, LT.-COL. A. D. LOGANATHAN, LT.-COL. EHSAN QADIR, LT.-COL. SHAH NAWAZ *(Representatives of the Armed Forces);*

A. M. SAHAY, *Secretary (with Ministerial Rank);*

RASH BEHARI BOSE *(Supreme Adviser);*

KARIM GIANI, DEBNATH DAS, D. M. KHAN, A. YELLAPPA, J. THIVY, SARDAR ISHAR SINGH *(Advisers);*

A. N. SARKAR *(Legal Adviser).*

SINGAPORE, *Oct. 21, 1943.*

***

Oath taken by Netaji on the proclamation of the establishment of the Provisional Government of Azad Hind:[64]

> In the name of God, I take this sacred oath that to liberate India and the thirty-eight crores of my countrymen, I, Subhas Chandra Bose, will continue the sacred war of freedom till the last breath of my life.

I shall remain always a servant of India and to look after the welfare of thirty-eight crores of Indian brothers and sisters shall be for me my highest duty.

Even after winning freedom, I will always be prepared to shed even the last drop of my blood for the preservation of India's Freedom.

* * *

Oath taken by the ministers of the Provisional Government on the occasion of the proclamation:[65]

In the name of God, I take this holy oath that to liberate India and the thirty-eight crores of my countrymen I, ..., will be absolutely faithful to my Leader Subhas Chandra Bose and shall be always prepared to sacrifice my life and all I have for fulfilling this pledge.

SONGS

The National Anthem of the Azad Hind Government

Shubh sukh chain ki barkha barse

Written in Hindustani—Netaji's preferred common language for Free India—by Mumtaz Hussein and Major Abid Hasan, this song was inspired by Tagore's Bengali poem '*Bharoto Bhagyo Bidhata*'—the first stanza of which later became the national anthem of the Republic of India. The music for '*Shubh sukh chain*' was composed by Captain Ram Singh Thakur. The version included in Asha-san's diary differs slightly from other versions, altered perhaps by memory or by the oral tradition through which it was passed down. The translation below is true to Asha-san's memory.

Shubh sukh chain ki varsha[66] *barse,*
Bharat bhagya hai jaga;

Punjab, Sindh, Gujarat, Maratha,
Dravid, Utkal, Banga,
chanchal sagar, Bindhya, Himachal,
neela Jamuna, Ganga.

Tere nit gun gayein,
tujhse jeevan payein,
sab tan payein asha.
Suraj ban kar jug par chamke,
Bharat naam subhaaga.
Jaya ho, jaya ho, jaya ho,
jaya, jaya, jaya, jaya ho!

Sab ke dil mein prati basein teri meethi baani,
har sube ke rahne wale, har mazhab ke prani,
sab bhedon farak mita ke,
sab god mein teri aake
goonthen prem ki mala.
Suraj ban kar jug par chamke,
Bharat naam subhaaga.
Jaya ho, jaya ho, jaya ho,
jaya, jaya, jaya, jaya ho!

Subah savere pankh pakheru,
tere hi gun gayein,
bas bhari bhar pankh hawaen
jeewan mein ritu layein,
sab mil kar Hind pukare,
jai Azad Hind ke nare.
Pyara desh hamara.
Suraj ban kar jug par chamke,
Bharat naam subhaaga.

Jaya ho, jaya ho, jaya ho,
jaya, jaya, jaya, jaya ho.

May the rains of auspiciousness and joy fall,
as India awakens to her destiny;
on Punjab, Sindh, Gujarat, Maharashtra,
on South India, Orissa, and Bengal,
on the restless seas, and
on the mountains of the Vindhyas and the Himachals,
and on the blue Yamuna and the Ganga.

We sing your eternal praises,
deriving life from you,
and fulfilling all our earthly hopes.
Like the sun, you shine over the world,
bringing fortune to India's name.
May victory be yours!

May your sweet voice grow in our hearts,
bringing us together, from every province, every religion.
Erasing all differences,
we gather in your lap
to string together a rosary of love.
Like the sun, you shine upon earth,
bringing fortune to India's name.
May victory be yours!

May the morning birds flutter their wings,
singing your song alone,
and may a full-feathered breeze,[67]
bring the seasons to life.
Let us join together

for our beloved nation, and chant:
'May Azad Hind be victorious!'
Like the sun, you shine upon earth,
bringing fortune to India's name.
May victory be yours!

* * *

The Marching Song of the Indian National Army

Kadam kadam barhaye ja

Written by Pandit Vanshidhar Shukla with music by Ram Singh Thakur, '*Kadam kadam barhaye ja*' served as the marching song of the INA. Asha-san, too, used to sing this song while marching with her platoon in the RJR. At the end of the war, the song was banned by the British Government till August 1947 for its seditious content. Post-independence, it continues to be the regimental quick march of the Indian Army.

Kadam kadam barhaye ja,
khushi ke geet gaye ja,
yeh zindagi hai qaum ki,
tu qaum pe lutaye ja.

Tu sher-e-hind aage barh,
marne se tu kabhi na darh,
urha ke dushmanon ke sar,
josh-e-watan barhaye ja.

Himmat teri barhti rahe,
khuda teri sunta rahe,
jo samne tere chareh,

tu khaq mein milaye ja.

Chalo Dilli pukar ke,
qaumi-nishan sambhal ke,
Lal Qile pe garh ke,
lahraye ja, lahraye ja.
Yeh zindagi hai qaum ki,
tu qaum pe lutaye ja.

Step by step, keep marching on,
singing songs of happiness,
your life belongs to the nation
and so lay it down for the nation.

Lion of India, march ahead,
may you never fear death,
by blowing off the enemy's head,
raise the spirits of the nation.

May your courage forever rise,
and may God always be by your side,
and those who stand in your way,
may you turn them into dust.

'Onwards to Delhi' on your lips,
cradling the flag of the nation,
plant it on the Red Fort,
where it will flutter, where it will fly.
Your life belongs to the nation
and so lay it down for the nation.

* * *

Subhasji, Subhasji

Written by Mumtaz Hussain and the Indian residents of Southeast Asia with music by Captain Ram Singh Thakur, this song welcomed Netaji on his arrival to Singapore on 2 July 1943.

Vah jaan-e-Hind aa gayein,
vah naaz jisne Hind ka
vah shaan-e-Hind aa gayein.

Subhas jaan-e-Hind hai,
Subhas aan-e-Hind hai.
Kali kali kali pe andleep chha rahi,
gali gali gali gali mein
khul ke aam aa rahi.

Vah shaan-e-Hind layenge,
vah aan-e-Hind layenge,
Amrikaon ke fauj par
vah kanhar banke chhayenge,
chaman ka phool khil gayein,
shobha ki kaliyan khuli.

Subhasji, Subhasji,
Asia ke aftaab,
Asia pe chha gaya.
Subhasji, Subhasji,
vah jaan-e-Hind aa gayein,
naaz jispe Hind ka
vah shaan-e-Hind aa gayein!
Jai Hind.

The life of India has arrived,
the pride of India,
the glory of India has arrived.

Subhas is the life of India,
Subhas brings dignity to India.
In each and every bud, incandescence glows,
in each and every lane, freedom gathers.
He will bring glory to India,
he will bring dignity to India.
He will unleash a pall of destruction
on American forces,
our flower gardens will bloom,
and our radiant buds will blossom.

Subhasji, Subhasji,
The sun of Asia
has risen over Asia.
Subhasji, Subhasji,
The life of India has arrived,
the pride of India,
the glory of India has arrived!
Jai Hind.

***

Qaumi Geet 1

A nationalistic song written by soldiers of the INA to inspire patriotism among their comrades, battling on the Indo-Burmese front.

Aansoon bharke aankhon mein,
sada ek geet gaata hoon,
mere Bharat, mere Bharat pe
deevana hoon, main deevana.

Kaaba hai tu-uski,
shivalya hai toh tu uski,
khuda tujhko bana baitha hai
abh yeh tera deevana.

Sotein khwab tu aayein,
jagtein dhyaan teri hai,
mandir ho ya masjid ho,
tumhein hi pata hai har deevana.

Jahan dekhe teri soorat,
jahan dhoonde teri moorat,
teri hi geet ga ga kar
sada rona hai tere devana.

Agar koi Hind ko jao to
yeh paigam le jana.

Eyes filled with tears,
I forever sing one song:
India, my India,
I am a lover, a lover.

If there is a Kaaba, then you are hers,
if there is a Shivalya, then you are hers,[68]
God has made you,
now you are her lover.

Asleep, I dream of you,
awake, I focus on you,
be it a temple or a mosque,
only you know every lover.

Wherever I look, your face,
wherever I search, your idol.
Singing your song alone
I cry forever, your lover.
If any of you go to India,
take this message with you.

* * *

Qaumi Geet 2

A poem written by Anand Mohan Sahay welcoming Pandit Jawaharlal Nehru to Pearl Hill Prison, Singapore, on 19 March 1945.

E-Hind ke Jawahar swagat tumhein hamara.
Bharat ke lal aao, swagat tumhein hamara.
Tumne humein sikhaya sewa watan ka karna
aafat museebaton ko huske sehatein rahna.
Tumhi se humne seekha hai jail ka yeh jeevan.

Hum qaid mein pade hai,
dil hai magar watan mein.
Bharat ke hum hai bacchein,
Bharat ka khoon hai tan mein.

Asha hai humein dil mein,
azad Hind ko karna.

Harkiz na chain leyenge,
jab tak jaan tan mein.

Samvad yeh hamara mata ke ja sunana,
Bharat na rah sakega harkiz gulaam khana.
Darkar ho agar phir nadiyan bahengi khoon ki,
taiyar hai hum baithe harkiz bhool na jaana.
E-Hind ke Jawahar swagat tumhein hamara.

Jewel of India, we welcome you.[69]
Patriot of India, come, we welcome you.
You taught us how to serve our nation,
to bear difficulties with a smile.
From you we have learnt this life of imprisonment.

We lie here in jail,
our country in our hearts.
We are the children of India,
India's blood flows through our veins.

Wishes flow through our hearts,
free India, we must.
We won't be at peace
till there is life in our bodies.

Tell this conversation to our mothers,
India will not remain a home of slaves.
If there is a need, rivers will flow with blood,
we are ready, don't ever forget.
Jewel of India, we welcome you.

NOTES

The Setting

1 Readers will find Anand Mohan Sahay's memoir *Stirring Times: An Autobiography of a Nationalist* an engrossing read.

The Sahay Family

2 The Azad Hind government is also known as the Provisional Government of Free India, or the Arzi Hukumat-e-Azad Hind.

Part One

3 Imperial Hotel was designed by the American architect Frank Lloyd Wright; it was considered one of his finest works. The hotel survived the 1923 Great Kantō earthquake and severe American bombing during the war. However, its foundations were damaged, and the hotel was demolished in 1967 and reconstructed as a high-rise. The front façade of the hotel has

been preserved and can be viewed in the Meiji Mura architectural museum near Nagoya.

4 The Hindi diary mentions Satyadev Sahay arriving in Japan in 1938 when Asha-san was ten years old. According to family sources, however, he arrived in 1930 at the age of nineteen.

5 Purani Sarai is the ancestral village of the Sahays, located in rural Bihar. Most women from upper-class Hindu families in the region observed purdah, the social practice of female segregation, covering their heads with the loose ends of their sarees in the presence of men.

6 Netaji had chosen Hindustani to be the common language of India. Hugh Toye mentions this in *Subhash Chandra Bose: The Springing Tiger*, p. 98: 'Bose had always held that the distinction between Hindi and Urdu was artificial. He advocated the adoption of the Roman Script as a means of integration and to simplify India's relations with the rest of the world.'

7 The Hindi diary does not specify where Baby and Ashok were evacuated to. Baby's daughter, Smita Sinha, clarified in 2021: 'They were evacuated up north to Niigata-ken and spent months in a Buddhist temple built inside a hill near a pine forest, along with their schoolmates.'

8 The Hikari Kikan served as the primary liaison and intelligence office between the INA/Azad Hind Government and the Imperial Japanese Army.

9 The oath attributed to Netaji in the Hindi diary differs slightly from other recorded versions.

10 The Hindi diary mentions Prime Minister Pibul Songgram (Plaek Phibunsongkhram) representing Thailand at the Greater East Asia Conference, whereas in reality Prince Wan Waithayakon represented the country. This was done in order to emphasize Thailand's status as an independent kingdom.

11 There is some ambiguity on the date of Netaji's arrival in the Andaman and Nicobar Islands. Hugh Toye's *The Springing Tiger* mentions this date as 29 December 1943 (p. 102). S.A. Ayer's *Unto Him a Witness* (p. xxix) mentions the date as 31 December 1943.

12 Netaji's Azad Hind Dal or Free India Group was an organization established to take charge of civil administration in Free India.

13 The Hindi diary mentions the date of this entry as 16 July 1943. As discussed in the Translator's Note, the Tokyo Boys arrived in

Japan in 1944. Moreover, Asha-san mentions the day of the week being a Sunday, matching 16 July 1944.

14 The Hindi diary mentions the total number of cadets as fifty. In reality, forty-five young men were selected for the training programme in Japan, joining both the Imperial Japanese Army Academy and the Imperial Japanese Army Air Academy.

15 The speech at Tokyo University took place in November 1944. The Hindi diary mentions this event as taking place in October 1944.

16 The failure of the Battle of Imphal, according to Netaji and his ministers, could partially be attributed to the substandard performance of the Hikari Kikan, both as a liaison office and in its inability to provide adequate weapons, rations and medical supplies to the INA.

17 The Hindi diary mentions this location as 'Mirjapur'. This is most likely a typographical error and the correct location is Manipur.

18 There is no date mentioned in this section of the Hindi diary. We can infer it is the early months of 1945 by the weather and the description of the air raids. American B-29 bombers began frequent raids over Tokyo from October 1944 onwards. The worst attacks, including incendiary firebombing, happened in February and March 1945.

19 American B-29 bombers were normally accompanied by fighter planes, most likely Grumman F6F Hellcats. The dogfights Asha-san witnessed were possibly between American Hellcats and Japanese Mitsubishi A6M Zeroes.

20 The Hindi diary mentions the date of this entry and the following entry as 25 February 1945. This could be a typographical error. In 1945, 25 February was a day of heavy incendiary bombing over Tokyo by B-29 bombers. It is unlikely that Asha-san would mention this date without mentioning the bombs.

21 Asha-san mentions Matsushita-san as her best friend in this section. However, the photographs that were taken on this day were with Suzuki-san. Both were good friends, according to Asha in 2022, and she finds it difficult to say who was the best.

22 Date changed from 25 February 1945 to end-February to maintain chronology.

23 Date changed from 21 February 1945 to maintain chronology.

24 This section was not included in the Hindi diary. It is based on the written recollections of Asha-san, shared with the translator in 2018.

25 There is a letter from Sati Sahay to Rabindranath Tagore dated 21 February 1939, where Sati requests Gurudev for accommodation in Santiniketan for herself and her two younger children. She states she does not have much money and, after living in Japan for so long, cannot imagine living in a city like Calcutta. The letter was written on board the *SS Tilawa* and has been translated from Bengali to English by Dr Supriya Roy. The return addressee is Dr S.C. Gupta.

26 The Hindi diary mentions Yonehara as a stop in between Tokyo and Kobe. This has been removed as Yonehara is east of Tokyo, while Kobe is to the southwest.

Part Two

27 This section of the Hindi diary has been augmented based on the recollections of Asha-san, recorded in 2018. In the Hindi diary, Sati Sahay carries a sewing kit with her while visiting the three Indian houses. In the 2018 version and in the oral stories she narrates, Asha-san mentions Sati carrying a matchbox with her.

28 A formal word for 'young lady' in Japanese.

29 Tokkotai is an abbreviation of 'tokubetsu kogekitai' meaning 'special attack units'.

30 Asha-san was often referred to as Asako, a common Japanese given name. 'Dono' is an honorific similar to 'san'.

31 Lin Shi's name was spelt as Rinshi in the Hindi diary. The translator had several dreams about Rinshi's mysterious palace before she located Lin Shi and the Wufeng Lin Family Mansion in Taichung, matching Asha-san's description.

32 The practice of taking modified 'French baths' continues in the Choudhry household till today. Asha-san's grandson and four-year-old great-grandson often wash their hands, feet and faces in the evening, apply some cologne, and triumphantly exclaim that they have just had a French bath.

33 Most likely the city of Kampong Cham in eastern Cambodia.

34 The permanent airbase, in the Hindi diary, is situated 200 miles from Bangkok. This is most likely a typographical error since the travel time from the airbase to Bangkok by car is about an hour.

The translator has estimated the distance to be twenty miles, or approximately thirty kilometres.

35 This road is called 'Vidyut Marg' in the Hindi diary. In letters written by Anand Mohan Sahay, he states the address as '122, Wireless Road, Bangkok'.

36 Kesra Devi Sharma, referred to as Mataji, was the wife of Pandit Raghunath Sharma.

37 Rasammah Navarednam's elder sister was Ponnammah, not Janaki Bai as mentioned in the Hindi diary.

38 Pandit Madhav Shukla was a poet, dramatist and Sanskrit scholar. He was also a patriot who wrote several books and poems supporting India's freedom struggle. The song '*Meri mata ke sar pe taj rahe*' was banned by the British government for its inciting content.

39 The lyrics of the song noted by Asha-san in her diary differ from other versions, including the popular version sung by Vasant Amrit of Surat.

40 The dates from end-June 1945 to August 1945 become ambiguous in the Hindi diary. The date 29 June 1945 is repeated twice and is then followed by an entry from 24 July 1945. The chronology also breaks after this, moving back and forth in time. The translator has edited specific dates into month-long ranges.

41 In the Hindi diary, Asha-san first says that she is touching the diary after twenty-five days and then two paragraphs later says she is touching the diary after a month and a half. The translator has estimated this to be one month.

42 Most likely Lt Ved Prakash Bhatia of the INA.

43 Netaji made several trips between Bangkok, Singapore and Seremban from June to August 1945. Asha-san mentions meeting Netaji in Bangkok on 23 July 1945. However, according to S.A. Ayer's *Unto Him a Witness*, Netaji was in Singapore on this date. To avoid confusion, I am mentioning only the month in this version of the diary.

44 In the Hindi diary, this entry comes before the meeting with Netaji. However, the decision to move the Ranis to Sacred Heart Convent took place when Netaji was present. Hence, the chronology has been edited.

45 In the Hindi diary, the date of the first bombing is mentioned as 5 August 1945.

46 Asha-san's Hindi translation of Emperor Hirohito's statement does not match other available statements. However, since Asha-

san uses quotes in her Hindi diary, it is possible that the words may have changed in her translation from Japanese to Hindi. The version used in this book is true to Hindi diary.

47 This passage begins with a quotation by Pandit Raghunath Sharma, but thereafter, quotation marks are missing. It is evident that Panditji is still speaking, so the translator has added quotation marks. Also, Netaji's speech on 15 August in the Hindi diary differs from available texts. It is possible that Panditji paraphrased. The version used in this book is true to Asha-san's Hindi diary.

48 The Hindi diary mentions the date of Netaji's death as 17 August 1945, instead of 18 August 1945.

Part Three

49 Months added by the translator based on dates mentioned in Anand Mohan Sahay's memoir.

50 In the Hindi diary, General Lu Han's name is spelt La-Han and Lohan interchangeably.

51 Also known as Outram Prison or Pearl's Hill Prison.

52 According to Anand Mohan Sahay's memoir, the commissioner at the time was Gar Chetur, an Indian Civil Service (ICS) officer.

53 The Hindi diary incorrectly names the hotel as Hotel Adelay.

54 The date of departure from Japan has been updated based on an interview with Sumona Varma (Baby) in 2021.

55 The last section of the diary has been restructured based on the recollections of Asha-san, recorded in 2018 while visiting the translator in Bangalore.

56 S.A. Ayer describes his stay with the Sahays in his book *Unto Him a Witness*, which begins as a comedy of errors. Ayer narrates (pp. 104–05): 'It seems that as soon as Rama Murti knew that I had arrived in Tokyo, he decided that I should be put up in Shri Sahay's house. So, before coming to the hotel to take me to Sahay's house, Rama Murti went up to Mrs Sahay and said to her: "Mrs Sahay, would you mind putting up Mr Ayer upstairs?" Mrs Sahay misheard what Rama Murti said and snapped out a most emphatic: "No. I shall never put him up. What do you mean by asking me to put up *that* man?" Poor Rama Murti was aghast at, what he thought, the shocking attitude of Mrs Sahay.'

It turns that Sati Sahay mistook Ayer for an unsavoury character and was characteristically vocal about her opinion.

57 Corrected from the 'end of September', which is most likely a typographical error in the Hindi diary. According to Ayer's *Unto Him a Witness*, Colonel Habib ur Rahman arrived in Tokyo on 6 September 1945.

58 The Hindi diary states the name of the INA cadet as Madhyapan. It is mostly likely either Cadet Nachiappan or Cadet Meiyappan.

59 This section is based on the recollections of Asha-san, recorded in 2018 while visiting the translator in Bangalore.

Character Sketches

60 These character sketches have been updated in 2021.

61 Since most records of the INA were destroyed in 1945, estimates of the total strength of the force and those killed in action vary. The figures mentioned here are from Prasenjit K. Basu's *Asia Reborn: A Continent Rises from the Ravages of Colonialism and War to a New Dynamism* (pp. 374–86).

62 S.A. Ayer's *Unto Him a Witness* (p. 55) describes Netaji's armed convoy driving from Seremban to Singapore in 1945 after the atom bombs had fallen. Satya Sahay's car brought up the rear and his luggage-carrier was overflowing with bananas—hard to find in Singapore then—including some overripe ones. Netaji cracked several jokes at Satya's expense en route.

Proclamation of the Provisional Government of Azad Hind (Free India)

63 Reproduced from S.A. Ayer's *Unto Him a Witness* (pp. 303–06).

64 Reproduced from S.A. Ayer's *Unto Him a Witness* (p. 306).

65 Ibid.

Songs

66 In the first line, Asha-san uses the word 'varsha' instead of 'barkha', which does not alter the meaning of the line.

67 Asha-san uses the words 'bhar pankh' (full-feathered) instead of 'bharpoor' (plenty).

68 Kaaba is the most sacred site in Islam, while Shivalya is a temple dedicated to the Hindu deity Shiva.

69 The word 'Jawahar' in Hindi means 'jewel' and refers to Jawaharlal Nehru, the Congress leader who visited Singapore in March 1946. Nehru laid a wreath at the site of the INA memorial during his visit and also spent time meeting INA prisoners of war in Pearl Hill Prison, including Anand Mohan Sahay. Sahay and the others were released a few weeks later on 30 March 1946.

BIBLIOGRAPHY

Ayer, S.A., *Unto Him a Witness: The Story of Netaji Subhas Chandra Bose in East Asia,* Bombay: Thacker and Co, 1951.

Ayer, S.A., *Story of the INA*, New Delhi: National Book Trust, 2002.

Basu, Prasenjit K., *Asia Reborn: A Continent Rises from the Ravages of Colonialism and War to a New Dynamism*, New Delhi: Aleph Book Company, 2017.

Benegal, Ramesh S., *Burma to Japan with Azad Hind: A War Memoir 1941-1945*, Atlanta, Georgia: Lancer Publishers, 2013.

Bose, Madhuri, *The Bose Brothers and Indian Independence: An Insider's Account*, New Delhi: Sage Publications, 2016.

Bose, Sisir Kumar, *Subhas and Sarat: An Intimate Memoir of the Bose Brothers*, New Delhi: Aleph Book Company, 2016.

Bose, Subhas Chandra, *Chalo Delhi: Writing and Speeches, 1943-1945,* eds: Sisir Kumar Bose and Sugata Bose, Calcutta: Netaji Research Bureau, 2007.

Bose, Subhas Chandra, *Selected Speeches of Subhas Chandra Bose*, New Delhi: Ministry of Information and Broadcasting, Government of India, 2013.

Bose, Subhas Chandra, *Netaji and the INA*, ed: Dr R.C. Bhardwaj, New Delhi: Lok Sabha Secretariat, 1994.

Bose, Sugata, *His Majesty's Opponent: Subhas Chandra Bose and India's Struggle against Empire*, Gurugram, India: Penguin Random House India, 2011.

Chhabra, Sagari, *In Search of Freedom: Journeys through India and South-East Asia*, Noida, India: HarperCollins Publishers India, 2015.

Chatterji, A.C., *India's Struggle for Freedom*, Calcutta: Chuckervertty, Chatterjee & Co, 1947.

Fay, Peter Ward, *The Forgotten Army: India's Armed Struggle for Independence 1942-1945*, New Delhi: Rupa Publications, 2020.

Gordon, Leonard A., *Brothers Against the Raj: A Biography of Indian Nationalists Sarat and Subhas Chandra Bose*, New Delhi: Rupa and Co, 1997.

Hildebrand, Vera, *Women at War: Subhas Chandra Bose and the Rani of Jhansi Regiment*, New Delhi: HarperCollins India, 2006.

Khan, Shah Nawaz, *My Memories of I.N.A. and its Netaji*, Delhi: Rajkamal Publications, 1946.

Khan, Shah Nawaz, Prem Kumar Sahgal, and Gurbax Singh Dhillon, *The I.N.A. Heroes: Autobiographies of Maj. Gen. Shahnawaz, Col. Prem K. Sahgal, Col. Gurbax Singh Dhillon of the Azad Hind Fauj*, Lahore: Hero Publications, 1946.

Khandwala, Rama, *Jai Hind: The Story of Lt Rama Khandwala of Netaji Subhas Chandra Bose Azad Hind Fauj*, Mot-Mot Publishing, 2020.

Lebra, Joyce Chapman, *Women Against the Raj: The Rani of Jhansi Regiment*, Singapore: ISEAS Publishing, 2008.

Sahay, Anand Mohan, *Stirring Times: An Autobiography of a Nationalist*, Calcutta: Purple Peacock Books & Arts, 2009.

Srivastav, Mahesh Prasad, *Videshi Bhumi Par Bhartiya Swadhinta Sangram*, New Delhi: Radha Publication, 2009.

Toye, Hugh, *Subhash Chandra Bose: The Springing Tiger*, Bombay: Jaico Publishing House, 1978.

ACKNOWLEDGEMENTS

To the many extraordinary people in my life, including Aiysha Jahan, Susmita Bhattacharya, Nazneen Ahmed, and the mentors and mentees of the British Council–funded Write Beyond Borders programme—for the masterclasses and words of inspiration.

To Saad Z. Hossain, Kanishka Gupta, Rahul Soni and the team at HarperCollins India for bringing this book to life.

To Sumona Varma, Vijaya Teelock, Neena Lallah, Smita Sinha, Mini Philips, Aman Varma, Pranav Bhatnagar, Shilpi Gulati, Kriti Gupta, Saumya Premchander, Sushmita Saha, Manjusha Chatterjee, Michelle Mirabella, Arpan Ganguli, Suneel Sinha, Miho Sakata Malhan, Naresh Dudlani and Rana Safvi—for sharing your knowledge with me.

To Samar and Leela—for teaching me how precious every moment is; Tanuj Choudhry, Ratna Choudhry, Smita Srivastava, Niraj Srivastava—early readers and early morning babysitters;

Sanjay Choudhry—for marching beside Asha-san for so many years and guiding this book to publication.

And, lastly, Bharati 'Asha' Sahay Choudhry—for your words and your indomitable spirit.

Tanvi Srivastava

ABOUT THE AUTHOR AND THE TRANSLATOR

Lt Bharati 'Asha' Sahay Choudhry was born in Kobe, Japan, in 1928 and joined the Rani of Jhansi Regiment of the Indian National Army at the age of seventeen. Her father, Anand Mohan Sahay, was a minister in the cabinet of the Azad Hind Government and a political adviser to Netaji Subhas Chandra Bose. Asha is currently ninety-four years old and lives in Patna with her son, Sanjay Choudhry, and her daughter-in-law, Ratna.

Tanvi Srivastava is a writer of fiction and has published short stories both online and in print. She is also a travel entrepreneur specializing in African expeditions. Tanvi is married to Asha's grandson and lives in Bangalore with her two wild children.

HarperCollins *Publishers* India

At HarperCollins India, we believe in telling the best stories and finding the widest readership for our books in every format possible. We started publishing in 1992; a great deal has changed since then, but what has remained constant is the passion with which our authors write their books, the love with which readers receive them, and the sheer joy and excitement that we as publishers feel in being a part of the publishing process.

Over the years, we've had the pleasure of publishing some of the finest writing from the subcontinent and around the world, including several award-winning titles and some of the biggest bestsellers in India's publishing history. But nothing has meant more to us than the fact that millions of people have read the books we published, and that somewhere, a book of ours might have made a difference.

As we look to the future, we go back to that one word—a word which has been a driving force for us all these years.

Read.